# African American Folklore

Lucent Library of Black History

**Other titles in this series:**

# African American Folklore

## Lucent Library of Black History

Stephen Currie

**LUCENT BOOKS**

*A part of Gale, Cengage Learning*

GALE
CENGAGE Learning™

Detroit • New York • San Francisco • New Haven, Conn • Waterville, Maine • London

## GALE
### CENGAGE Learning™

*In memory of my father, David P. Currie, 1936–2007,
who loved the Br'er Rabbit stories, told them as often
as possible, and made them truly his own.*

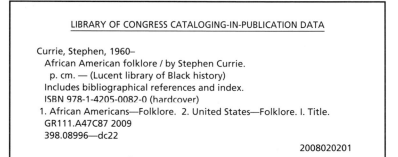

LIBRARY OF CONGRESS CATALOGING-IN-PUBLICATION DATA

Currie, Stephen, 1960–
    African American folklore / by Stephen Currie.
        p. cm. — (Lucent library of Black history)
    Includes bibliographical references and index.
    ISBN 978-1-4205-0082-0 (hardcover)
    1. African Americans—Folklore. 2. United States—Folklore. I. Title.
    GR111.A47C87 2009
    398.08996—dc22
                                                        2008020201

Lucent Books
27500 Drake Rd.
Farmington Hills, MI 48331

ISBN-13: 978-1-4205-0082-0
ISBN-10: 1-4205-0082-1

Printed in the United States of America
3 4 5 6 7 13 12 11 10 09

Printed by Bang Printing, Brainerd, MN, 3rd Ptg., 10/2009

# Contents

# Foreword

It has been more than 500 years since Africans were first brought to the New World in shackles, and over 140 years since slavery was formally abolished in the United States. Over 50 years have passed since the fallacy of "separate but equal" was obliterated in the American courts, and some 40 years since the watershed Civil Rights Act of 1965 guaranteed the rights and liberties of all Americans, especially those of color. Over time, these changes have become celebrated landmarks in American history. In the twenty-first century, African American men and women are politicians, judges, diplomats, professors, deans, doctors, artists, athletes, business owners, and home owners. For many, the scars of the past have melted away in the opportunities that have been found in contemporary society. Observers such as Peter N. Kirsanow, who sits on the U.S. Commission of Civil Rights, point to these accomplishments and conclude, "The growing black middle class may be viewed as proof that most of the civil rights battles have been won."

In spite of these legal victories, however, prejudice and inequality have persisted in American society. In 2003, African Americans comprised just 12 percent of the nation's population, yet accounted for 44 percent of its prison inmates and 24 percent of its poor. Racially motivated hate crimes continue to appear on the pages of major newspapers in many American cities. Furthermore, many African Americans still experience either overt or muted racism in their daily lives. A 1996 study undertaken by Professor Nancy Krieger of the Harvard School of Public Health, for example, found that 80 percent of the African American participants reported having experienced racial discrimination in one or more settings, including at work or school, applying for housing and medical care, from the police or in the courts, and on the street or in a public setting.

It is for these reasons that many believe the struggle for racial equality and justice is far from over. These episodes of discrimination threaten to shatter the illusion that America has completely overcome its racist past, causing many black Americans to become increasingly frustrated and confused. Scholar and writer Ellis Cose has described this splintered state in the following way: "I have done everything I was supposed to do. I have stayed out of trouble with the law, gone to the right schools, and worked myself nearly to death. What more do they want? Why in God's name won't they accept me as a full human being?" For Cose and others, the struggle for equality and justice has yet to be fully achieved.

In many subtle yet important ways the traumatic experiences of slavery and segregation continue to inform the way race is discussed and experienced in the twenty-first century. Indeed, it is possible that America will always grapple with the fallout from its distressing past. Ulric Haynes, dean of the Hofstra University School of Business, has said, "Perhaps race will always matter, given the historical circumstances under which we came to this country." But studying this past and understanding how it contributes to present-day dialogues about race and history in America is a critical component of contemporary education. To this end, the Lucent Library of Black History offers a thorough look at the experiences that have shaped the black community and the American people as a whole. Annotated bibliographies provide readers with ideas for further research, while fully documented primary and secondary source quotations enhance the text. Each book in the series explores a different episode of black history; together they provide students with a wealth of information as well as launching points for further study and discussion.

# Introduction

## Folklore and African Americans

The famous African American writer Zora Neale Hurston once described folklore as "the boiled-down juice of human living."[1] Another black American author, Ralph Ellison, agreed; he wrote that folklore was a way to "depict the humor as well as the horror"[2] of life. Indeed, folklore is central to the human experience. Every culture has a long and complex folk tradition. In each case, moreover, that folk tradition is important in two ways. First, it reflects the history and experiences of the people who created it. Second, it serves to hold these same people together by giving them a shared culture and a common way of making sense of the world.

The term *folklore* often brings to mind specific images and works, such as fairy tales, cowboy songs, or children's rhymes. In fact, though, folklore is broader than this picture would indicate. Folklore encompasses almost any stories, songs, or other spoken or written materials that are passed from one person to another. In the past, folklore has most often been spread orally—that is, by people who tell stories or sing songs to their friends and neighbors. Today, folklore can still be spread in this way. In a modern society, however, folklore is increasingly likely to reach new audiences through other means—most notably through books, through recordings, and even through e-mail, blogs, and text messages.

Not all written or spoken works qualify as folklore. For the most part, pieces that can be traced to a particular author or composer are not considered part of the folk tradition. Unlike true folklore, these works are static and unchanging. In contrast, folk rhymes, songs, and stories, which typically have no single creator, are always being altered through what is known as the folk process. As stories, songs, or riddles are passed from one person to another, they may be remembered imperfectly and retold in a slightly different way. Alternatively, tellers may decide to change older materials by setting a familiar lyric to a new melody, adding a scene to a folktale, or shortening the setup of a joke. In either case, the effect is the same: The work is changed, perhaps forever. This is the folk process at work.

"The test of any good folktale," writes author Virginia Hamilton, "is how long it stays in the minds of listeners and in circulation with tellers."[3] Stories and songs remain in circulation partly by being entertaining, but even more importantly, by connecting with the needs and desires of a group of people. Those who pass on folklore most often spread the works that speak most clearly to them. The songs and stories of a given people, then, usually reveal their deepest sorrows, their fondest hopes, and their most cherished dreams. As anthropologist Frantz Fanon puts it, "When a story flourishes in the heart of a folklore it is because in one way or another it expresses an aspect of the 'spirit of the group.'"[4] In this sense, the folk process connects the folklore of a culture to the soul of its people.

## Rich Folk Tradition

The folk tradition of African Americans has long been exceptionally rich and varied—and especially close to the hearts of American blacks. African American folklore ranges from stories about talking animals to barbed jokes about slave masters, from songs that tell of the struggle to survive in a difficult and broken world to tales of mythic black heroes and role models. The stories and songs of black Americans reveal the ways in which African Americans view the world around them—and how they view themselves as well.

An engraving depicts music, a key component of African American folklore, as welcome solace in the otherwise dreary daily life of slaves.

To African Americans, the folk tradition has provided many things over the years. Through music, in particular, folklore has offered blacks solace and strength in the face of sorrow and trouble—experiences well known to African Americans, given the long and brutal history of slavery and racism they have often encountered. Folklore has also helped black Americans to express joy, along with their assurance that someday, whether on earth or in the afterlife, they will enter a better world. And perhaps most important of all, folklore has given African Americans a collective body of traditions that has set them apart from other groups and has encouraged them to take pride in their history. In this way, folklore has helped African Americans build a strong and vibrant culture.

Finally, as folklorist Daryl Cumber Dance writes, folklore is particularly vital to African Americans because traditional history often ignores or minimizes the black experience. Many historical records simply do not exist for African Americans as they do for their white counterparts. Southern plantation owners, for example, often did not bother to note the births of slave children in any formal way. Nor did most blacks have last names until slavery came to an end. In addition, history has typically been told by the powerful, in ways that can ignore the contributions of others. In this case, white historians have often overlooked or downplayed the experiences of black Americans. In many standard American histories, as a result, African Americans have been a footnote or an afterthought.

Folklore, Dance argues, bridges that gap. Folk songs and folktales, she writes, present the thoughts and feelings of blacks in a way that traditional histories often cannot do. The stories told by former slaves, the songs of urban blacks in the early twentieth century, the verbal jousting of African American youths today—all of these represent genuine black voices. These voices can help blacks better understand their culture and guide others toward understanding it, too. As Dance writes, "Those truly interested in African American life and culture need to begin their quest for knowledge [by studying folklore]. . . . While folklore is an important source for the study of any group, it is critical and indispensable as a source in our consideration of the African American experience."[5]

## Chapter One

# African American Folk Stories

Folk stories are often regarded as being at the heart of folklore. Full-fledged narratives with characters, a setting, a plot, and occasionally a moral, folktales come in many different forms. A fairy tale is one type of folk story. Ghost stories, which describe the supernatural world, are another. Still other folktales are stories of talking animals, narratives that tell about life in the past, or legends loosely based on actual happenings. Folktales describe the actions of tricksters, of scoundrels, of spirits, and of ordinary human beings; they may be intended to teach, to amuse, to sadden, or to shock. The folk stories of African Americans are all these things and more. They are a vital part of the African American folk tradition.

## Animal Tales

Some of the best-known African American folktales are animal stories. Though a few animal tales are about real animals, these stories most often focus on talking creatures that act much more like people than like actual animals. For the most part, animals in African American folktales tend to be motivated by greed, jealousy, laziness, and other strongly human emotions and characteristics. These tales typically include no actual humans as characters, though there are exceptions. Most African American animal stories focus on foxes, chickens, frogs, and other creatures that are common in the American South.

Many animal stories are so-called *parce que* tales. This name is taken from the French word for "because"; these stories give fanciful explanations of why animals are the way they are. One African American story, for instance, explains why tadpoles become frogs. When God created the first tadpoles, or so the narrative runs, they were assigned to pull weeds in a field. The tadpoles disobeyed the order, however, and went swimming instead. As punishment, God took away their tails. When the tadpoles protested, God offered them legs. The legs, God pointed out, would allow the tadpoles to swim while reminding them that "there was something else to do in this world other than swimming." That settled the issue. "And to this day," the story concludes, "you notice that a tadpole, when he grows up, he loses his tail, gets legs, and turns into a frog."[6]

The most famous African American animal stories, though, are a set of tales that describe the adventures of a character known as Br'er Rabbit. (Sometimes the name is given as "Bruh" or "Buh" Rabbit; all are shortened forms of "Brother," a term frequently used during the 1800s by African American men when they addressed one another.) The Br'er Rabbit tales are set in a landscape similar to the forests of the South. They include a wide cast of animal characters, such as Br'er Bear, Br'er Turtle, and Sister Alligator. However, the focus of most of the stories is Br'er Rabbit himself and his relationship with his longtime enemies, Br'er Fox and Br'er Wolf. Smaller and weaker than these predators, Br'er Rabbit can only survive in the forest by using his wits.

## Br'er Rabbit and Friends

Many of the Br'er Rabbit stories, accordingly, describe how Br'er Rabbit outsmarts his enemies. In the story "The Talking House," for example, Br'er Wolf sneaks into Br'er Rabbit's house while the rabbit is out. Br'er Wolf then hides; he plans to jump out and catch Br'er Rabbit when he hears the door open again. However, Br'er Wolf leaves the front door slightly ajar, and Br'er Rabbit notices this upon his return. Suspecting a trap, he develops a plan of his own to flush out Br'er Wolf. Instead of going inside, Br'er Rabbit

Among the best-known African American folktales are those that tell of the adventures of wily Br'er Rabbit and his encounters with other forest creatures.

starts speaking to the house as if it is alive. "Hey, house!" he yells in Julius Lester's 1987 retelling of the tale. "How you doing today?"[7]

At first, Br'er Wolf stays silent. But as Br'er Rabbit begins berating the house for not answering him, Br'er Wolf realizes that his prey will not come through the doorway unless the house responds. Br'er Wolf knows perfectly well that the house is not going to speak, so he disguises his voice and says something in return. He hopes that Br'er Rabbit, suspicions lulled, will now hop into the house. The opposite, of course, is true: The moment Br'er Wolf replies, Br'er Rabbit knows who is speaking. "Brer Wolf!" he calls. "You got to do some practicing if you want to talk like a house!"[8] Embarrassed, Br'er Wolf leaves the house. For the moment, at least, he gives up the chase.

Not all the Br'er Rabbit stories show the rabbit as the hero, however. Br'er Rabbit can also be a conniving trickster who taunts other animals, only to see his pranks backfire. In one story, Br'er Rabbit and Br'er Buzzard each plant crops and agree to split their harvests equally between them. Br'er Rabbit, however, has no intention of sharing. "Didn't a thing come up," he lies to Br'er Buzzard once the crops are ready for harvesting, "so I ain't got nothing to divide with you."[9] Suspecting that the rabbit is not telling the truth, Br'er Buzzard works out a trick of his own. He offers to give Br'er Rabbit a ride across a river. When the rabbit accepts, Br'er Buzzard flies to a pine tree on an island halfway across the

Featured in over one hundred separate tales, Br'er Rabbit is sometimes portrayed as a hero and other times as a trickster.

river—and leaves Br'er Rabbit there, clinging to the treetop, until he agrees to share his crops after all.

A few of the Br'er Rabbit narratives also function as *pourquoi* tales. One example is a story often referred to as "How Mr. Rabbit Lost His Fine Bushy Tail." In this narrative, Br'er Rabbit is described as having a beautiful long tail, unlike the rabbits of today. One day, though, Br'er Rabbit meets up with Br'er Fox, who has just caught a large number of fish. Intrigued, Br'er Rabbit asks the fox how he managed to catch so many. Br'er Fox explains that he simply hung his tail down into the river all night long and waited for fish to latch onto it. Though the night is cold, Br'er Rabbit decides to try it himself. Unfortunately, when he goes to lift his tail out of the water at dawn, the water has frozen solid. "He make a pull," runs one version of the story, "en he feel like he comin' in two, en he fetch nudder [another] jerk, en lo en beholes, whar wuz his tail?"[10] It had pulled right off, the story explains, and that is why rabbits have small tails today.

## Br'er Rabbit's Popularity

Br'er Rabbit stories have been popular among African Americans for at least two centuries. Folklorists have collected well over a hundred separate Br'er Rabbit tales from across most of the South, and nearly any collection of African American folklore features at least a few of these narratives. The stories were certainly known to blacks during the slave era. They first achieved a wider audience in the late 1800s, however, when Joel Chandler Harris, a white writer from Georgia, published dozens of Br'er Rabbit tales in a group of books about black folklore. Though the framing device Harris uses for his book—an elderly ex-slave telling the stories to a young white boy—has become distasteful to many modern readers, there is little doubt that Harris faithfully recorded the stories as he heard them from African American men and women. Since Harris's time, other authors and storytellers, black and white, have also published their own versions of the Br'er Rabbit tales.

One reason for the enduring popularity of these stories involves the plucky little rabbit himself. It is hard to dislike Br'er Rabbit, even when he is being greedy, foolish, or downright mean. Br'er Rabbit never gives up, never lets a defeat bother him for long, and always approaches life with a mocking sense of humor. He is cer-

Author Joel Chandler Harris collected and published dozens of popular Br'er Rabbit stories.

tainly among the more charming and best-developed characters in all of folklore. The stories about Br'er Rabbit and his companions are usually quite funny, too, making them enjoyable to tell, to listen to, and to read.

The Br'er Rabbit stories are also popular because they provide opportunities for storytellers to use language in interesting ways, to exaggerate for effect, and to experiment with different telling devices. Joel Chandler Harris's versions, taken more or less directly from former slaves, include vivid images such as "he skip out des ez [just as] lively ez a cricket in de embers"[11] and "feelin' des ez scrumpshus ez a bee-martin [a type of bird] wid a fresh bug."[12] A folklore collector of the early twentieth century recorded African American storytellers using lines such as, "It was a right bodacious plan, too, but then Brer Rabbit is a right bodacious creature."[13] More recent storytellers have also played with language and images. "Better look out for Bruh Rabbit when next the day leans over and night falls down,"[14] writes noted author Virginia Hamilton in her picture book retelling of one of the tales.

## Fairy Tales

Another class of African American folk stories is made up of fairy tales. Like the Br'er Rabbit tales, fairy tales sometimes include talking animal characters; however, they usually focus on humans rather than on animals. Many fairy tales feature clear battles between good and evil, generally—though not always—won by the forces of good, and they often include elements of magic. African American fairy tales are not as widely known today as their European counterparts, such as Hansel and Gretel, Cinderella, and Jack and the Beanstalk. Nonetheless, the African American tradition includes many compelling fairy tales with intricate plots and interesting characters.

One well-known African American fairy tale, for instance, is called "The Talking Eggs." This story tells of a pair of sisters, one good, the other bad. As in many European fairy tales, the bad sister is favored by the girls' mother. In the story, the good sister does several kindnesses for a mysterious woman who offers the girl some eggs as a reward. The eggs are talking eggs, the woman explains, and the sister should only take the eggs that say, "Take me." "When you are on the way home," the woman tells the girl, "throw the eggs behind you to break them."[15] The girl does as instructed, and the eggs turn into gold, diamonds, and beautiful dresses.

The girl's mother then sends her favored daughter out to locate the woman, expecting that she will get the same reward. But this sister is not so kind and not so obedient. She makes fun of the woman and criticizes her home and surroundings. When the woman tells the bad sister to take only those eggs that say, "Take me," the girl ignores the instruction and decides to bring home the eggs that say "Don't take me"[16] instead. On the way home, she

# Zora Neale Hurston

Born in Florida in 1891, Zora Neale Hurston had a long and successful career as a writer. She is best known today for a novel about rural African American life called *Their Eyes Were Watching God*, but Hurston wrote several other important novels as well. She also was one of the guiding lights of the Harlem Renaissance, a literary and artistic movement among blacks in New York City during the 1920s. Today, Hurston is considered among the greatest of all African American writers.

Among Hurston's many interests was folklore. In the late 1920s she traveled to the Deep South to seek out folktales, jokes, and other traditional lore of African Americans. She had ambitious plans for this material: She hoped to produce a seven-volume set of black American folklore, including volumes on stories, children's games, and love letters. Though Hurston collected huge amounts of material, she published only two of these proposed collections before moving on to other projects.

Author Zora Neale Hurston's research and collection of stories, jokes, and other materials in the late 1920s was instrumental in preserving the traditional lore of African Americans.

Over the years, the remainder of the material Hurston had collected disappeared. Years after her death, however, many of these stories resurfaced; they had been mixed in with the papers of an anthropologist at Columbia University in New York. In 2001 some of the stories were edited and published in a volume called *Every Tongue Got to Confess: Negro Folk-Tales from the Gulf States*. It is an excellent and valuable collection of folklore among African Americans of a particular time and place.

throws the eggs over her shoulder, expecting the same treasures as her sister got. In her case, however, the talking eggs turn into toads, snakes, and whips, which chase her all the way home—thus giving her the punishment she deserves.

Other African American fairy tales tell of romances and journeys. A Cinderella-type tale known as Catskinella describes how a young woman captures the heart of a prince with the aid of a magic mirror and a good-hearted godmother. Another tale, "The Beautiful Girl of the Moon Tower," is about a man named Anton who tries to find a woman who lives in a tower on the moon. While traveling, he helps various animals, including an eagle, an ant, and a lion. These creatures help him in return by helping him change into their forms as the occasion demands. To cover great distances, Anton becomes an eagle; to creep into small places, he becomes an ant; and to win a fight in the climactic scene of the story, he becomes a lion. In the end, Anton marries the woman in the tower, and they become king and queen of the moon.

## Supernatural Tales

Closely related to fairy tales in African American folklore are tales of the supernatural. These stories deal with the darker side of magic: specifically, with witches, ghosts, the devil, and other demons. Many of these stories, to be sure, are told for comic effect. In Virginia Hamilton's retelling of a tale known as "Better Wait Till Martin Comes," for example, a man named John finds himself in a mysterious house. Over a period of time, several black cats enter the house, each larger than the one before—and all of them eyeing John hungrily. "What you want to do with him there?" the largest of the cats finally asks the others, indicating John. "We better wait till Martin comes," they reply. Thoroughly alarmed, John races out of the house. "Mister Cats!" he calls back over his shoulder. "You tell Martin I was here, but I couldn't wait on [for] him. And now I'm gone!"[17]

Other supernatural tales show people outwitting the devil in ways reminiscent of Br'er Rabbit tricking his predators in African American animal stories. In one story from the Deep South, for example, the devil steals a girl out of her bed and holds her in his mouth as he flies off. The girl's mother dashes outside in a panic—but quickly sees how she can rescue her daughter. "Hey, old

## A Powerful Memory

A well-known African American folktale about the supernatural world tells about a slave named John who happened to have a powerful memory. The devil appears one day to John's owner and expresses his desire to take John with him to the underworld. The owner, however, objects. He describes the man's phenomenal memory and explains that this talent makes John invaluable to him in his work on the farm. "I can ask him about my crops and what I made last year," the owner says, "and how many bushels of corn and what have you, and John has the answer [snap of the finger] just like that."

The devil is intrigued by this description and agrees to leave John alone if his memory is as impressive as the owner claims. To test John's memory, the devil pops up in front of the slave one day and asks, "Do you like eggs?" When John answers yes, the devil immediately disappears. Two years later, though, the devil pops back up again and says the single word "How?" John unhesitatingly replies, "Scrambled."

Quoted in Daryl Cumber Dance, *From My People: 400 Years of African American Folklore.* New York. W.W. Norton, 2002, p. 49.

Satan," she calls, "is you comin back after more?"[18] The devil unthinkingly opens his mouth to answer, thereby releasing his grip on the girl. She tumbles safely to the ground and runs home.

But most African American tales of the supernatural are a good deal more serious than these examples. More often than not, these stories result in a victory for the demons. That is especially true when ordinary people foolishly call on evil spirits for help. In one tale, for instance, a slave named Balaam believes that his master will release him from slavery if Balaam becomes a virtuoso fiddle player. Balaam summons the devil, who appears in an ominous "black cloud full of smoke an' sulphur."[19] The two bargain, and the devil gives the slave the skills he seeks in exchange for his eternal soul. When Balaam's master hears Balaam play, he does indeed set the fiddler free. But in the long run, Balaam loses: The devil claims him when he dies.

Underestimating the power of the spirit world is another danger in these stories. One story deals with a boy named Little Eight John, who mocks the spirits by defying common African American superstitions. Told that it is bad luck to count the number of teeth he has, for instance, Little Eight John cheerfully counts his teeth; cautioned not to climb trees on Sundays, Little Eight John does precisely that. The spirits soon get their revenge. Little Eight John's siblings get sick, his parents lose their money, and Little

# Women in Folktales

Folktales from most traditions often share a certain characteristic: They are more likely to be about boys and men than about girls and women. The stories of African Americans are no exception. The heroes of supernatural stories such as "Tailypo" and "Little Eight John," for instance, are usually male. So are the masters and slaves featured in the John tales. And Br'er Rabbit, Br'er Fox, and the other animal characters in the Uncle Remus stories are overwhelmingly identified as male.

Even so, there are some African American folktales that do feature women. A few of these are described in the main text of this chapter. Annie Christmas, for example, is a woman. Likewise, the characters in "The Talking Eggs" are all female. Some African American folktales tell of mermaids or of "conjure women"—people believed capable of casting magic spells. Occasionally, girls are the main characters. Sometimes these girls are foolish, sometimes clever; sometimes, they are both at once. In one story, for instance, a girl foolishly promises the devil her soul, but she gets the last laugh years later when he comes to collect the soul she owes him—and receives instead the sole of her shoe.

In recent years there has been a surge of interest in folk stories about girls and women. A number of new folktale collections focus on stories of this type, including examples from the African American tradition. Among these, in particular, is an anthology called *Her Stories* by the noted American black writer Virginia Hamilton. This volume presents stories from African American folklore, each of which highlights at least one central female character; it is a valuable resource for anyone interested in the role of girls and women in black folklore.

Eight John is destroyed by a demon called Old Raw Head Bloody Bones. In another tale, a traveler named Tabb insists on staying the night in a haunted house. His decision backfires, however, when a spirit unexpectedly grabs him and tries to overpower him. Several of Tabb's friends do their best to pull him from the spirit's grip. In the end, though, the spirit is too strong; it pulls the unfortunate Tabb out of the building and away into the night. "Nothing was ever seen of [Tabb] again,"[20] the story concludes.

## Annie Christmas

A few African American folktales of the supernatural deal with heroes and heroines—black Americans who may or may not have existed. Some of these tales are familiar in two or even three different forms: as songs, as stories, and sometimes even as poems. In several cases, these heroes and heroines are better known through songs than through folk narratives. Others of these mythic figures, however, are known primarily through folktales. Among these is the legend of Annie Christmas of New Orleans.

Like many heroes of folklore, Annie Christmas is large, strong, and determined. She pilots a riverboat up and down the Mississippi; she has twelve strapping sons; she fights anyone who offends her, and she usually wins. "[Annie] stood seven feet barefoot," writes Virginia Hamilton in her 1995 version of the story, "and she weighed two-ninety-nine pound. . . . Men were stone scared of Annie 'cause she was tough."[21] But that rough exterior hides some very different emotions as well. According to the legend, Annie falls in love with a fellow captain, who wants nothing to do with her. Distraught, she curses him and jumps into the river to drown herself.

The captain is never seen again, or so the story goes. As for Annie, her body is found washed up along the banks of the Mississippi. Her sons prepare the body for burial and stage an elaborate funeral—attended, among others, by "all the men she'd beaten at hand-wrestling and fistfighting." Annie's sons then take her coffin aboard a black barge and float with it down the Mississippi toward the Gulf of Mexico. They are never seen again in the flesh; but their presence persists. "Annie Christmas is still on the big river around New Orleans-town," Hamilton writes in her conclusion to the tale. "The black barge comes out of the mist. Her twelve sons stand straight and tall. . . . And there's Annie, sitting on her own wood grave, singing a river tune to the thundering sky."[22]

# John Tales

Not all African American folktales deal with ghosts, talking rabbits, or magic mirrors. Among the more realistic African American folktales are the so-called John stories, which date to before the Civil War and typically feature a slave named John. In many of these stories, John is pitted against his master or an influential white man. Sometimes, John fools the master, Br'er Rabbit–style. In one tale, for instance, John arranges for a friend to carry items such as a bag of flour and a side of bacon up into a tree. John then tells his master that God will listen directly to him. He stands beneath the tree and asks for the items one by one, with the friend releasing the bags in the correct order. The master is fooled and believes that God is actually responsible. When John threatens to ask God to destroy all the white people, his master gives John his freedom instead, along with "forty acres an' uh thousand dollars."[23]

A similar story tells of a slave, this one named Jeff, who tries to join a white church. The preacher tells Jeff that blacks need to worship separately from whites. When Jeff wonders why, the preacher suggests that Jeff ask God for guidance on the issue. Jeff returns a few weeks later to tell the preacher how this discussion went. "[God] say dat a good Christian lak me oughter been 'shamed of myself for even comin' here thinkin' 'bout joinin' dis church," Jeff reports. But the preacher's approval upon hearing this turns to consternation as Jeff continues: "[God] say He ain't never even joined here hisself. Fact is, He don't think He could git in if He wuz to try."[24] This slave does not get his freedom, but he does manage a dig against the powerful whites who ran the pre–Civil War South.

Most John stories do not end so happily, however. The reality of slave life was that the masters held the upper hand, and the John tales often reflect that. In another John story, John finds a talking turtle. He rushes off to tell his master, who refuses to believe the story. Indeed, when John and his master arrive at the river, the turtle chooses to remain silent, and John is severely beaten for telling lies. Yet another John tale tells of a time when a slave was left in charge of his master's plantation while the master was away. Instead of making sure the work was done, the slave declared a holiday with dancing and games. The master, however, surprised the slave by coming back early. Like the slave in the turtle story, this slave was also punished.

Whether these stories deal with real people, the spirit world, or the conflicts between Br'er Rabbit and Br'er Fox, the African American folktale tradition is a long and proud one. Generations of American blacks have grown up knowing and cherishing these tales. They have brought laughter, romance, and sometimes a shiver of fear to African Americans all across the country—and whether through books, CDs, blogs, e-mails, or the swapping of stories on a front porch or in a minivan, they continue to do the same to an ever wider audience today. The folktales from the African American tradition will always speak to something deep inside people. "After all," writes author and folktale collector Julius Lester, "what is a tale except a means of expressing love for this experience we call being human[?]"[25]

## Chapter Two

# Folk Songs

Like stories, songs have long been an essential part of African American folklore. In some ways, indeed, music is the art form most closely associated with black Americans. Well before the Civil War, visitors to plantations across the American South were commenting on the slaves' musical skills and ability to express their emotions through song. Later, African Americans helped develop such notable musical styles as the blues, jazz, rock, and hip-hop. Religious and nonreligious songs alike have helped generations of African Americans play, work, love, and worship. More than that, the music of African Americans has helped blacks celebrate the joys and endure the hardships of their lives. The vitality of the African American musical tradition continues to thrive.

## Spirituals

Many of the best-known examples of African American folk music today are spirituals—deeply religious songs that deal with biblical themes, the afterlife, and the singer's relationship with God. Though the earliest slaves adhered to various tribal religions common in Africa, that began to change in the mid-1700s; by the early 1800s, most African Americans were at least nominally Christian. To be sure, the slaves' exposure to traditional Christian worship varied considerably. Whereas

some blacks were required by their owners to go to church ser-
vices, at the other extreme, a few masters forbade slaves from
formal worship altogether. But whether they could worship
openly or not, virtually all African American slaves could sing to
express their religious feelings—and a great many of them did
exactly that.

It is impossible to determine precisely when American blacks
started creating spirituals, but it is clear that some of these songs
date back to the mid-1700s, if not earlier. In general, though,
spirituals are associated most closely with the 1800s. They were
widespread in the South in the years before the Civil War and re-
tained their popularity for some time following the end of slavery.
Although spirituals fell out of favor by 1900 or so, the songs of
the 1800s remain familiar to many Americans, black and white,
even in the twenty-first century; and at least one pair of experts,
folk song collectors John and Alan Lomax, have written that spirituals "form the most impressive body of music so far produced
by America, ranking with the best of music anywhere on this
earth."[26]

Spirituals varied considerably. Many spirituals, perhaps most,
were introspective. Meant to be sung slowly and thoughtfully,
they functioned as an extended prayer or simply as a plaintive
cry to God. These spirituals often reflected the reality of life under slavery, in which blacks were brutalized and forced to labor
for no pay. "Every tone [of these songs] was a testimony against
slavery," writes Frederick Douglass, who grew up a slave and
later became a great antislavery orator, "and a prayer to God for
deliverance from chains."[27] Whether sung by individuals or by
a group, these songs were a way for African Americans to voice
their frustrations and sorrows. Indeed, spirituals of this type
were often known as "sorrow songs." "Sometimes I feel like a
motherless child," reads the text of one sorrow song, "a long way
from home."[28]

In contrast to the sorrow songs were spirituals that focused on
the Christian promise of a better life after death. Instead of dwell-
ing on the imperfections of the world as it was, these songs con-
centrated on the joy of entering heaven. "I'm gwine to my heaven,
I'm gwine home," says one song of this type, "Archangel[,] open

Slaves are depicted singing spirituals, which expressed both the sadness of their plight and the joy of their faith.

de door."[29] Emotionally, these songs were much more upbeat than the sorrow songs, and the music tended to reflect that as well. Though some of these more joyful spirituals were meant to be sung slowly, more of them had a lively beat and a quick tempo. The tunes alone, then, were often enough to distinguish these spirituals from the sorrow songs.

## Bible Stories

Other spirituals were musical retellings or reinterpretations of biblical stories. The spiritual "Joshua Fit [Fought] the Battle of Jericho," for instance, describes how the Israelite leader Joshua captured the city of Jericho by blowing a trumpet, thereby causing the city's walls to crumble. Others tell the story of Jacob, a figure in Genesis who wrestled with an angel; the prophet Ezekiel, who had a long and complex vision described in the Bible; and the creation of Adam and Eve. A few spirituals retold stories from the New Testament as well. As one spiritual about Jesus's crucifixion puts it, "Dey nailed him to de cross, an' he never said a mumblin' word."[30]

Of all the stories in the Bible, however, pre–Civil War blacks found themselves most drawn to the tale of the flight from Egypt. This narrative, appearing in the book of Exodus, describes how Moses led the Hebrew people out of slavery and toward the Promised Land. The story of Moses, naturally enough, had particular significance to the enslaved African Americans of the South. They longed for a Moses of their own, a figure who would appear in their own lives and lead them to freedom as well. Several spirituals were based on this story. The most famous of these today is "Go Down, Moses," the chorus of which reads:

> Go down, Moses,
> Way down in Egypt land
> Tell ole Pharaoh
> Let my people go.[31]

Spirituals that referenced the biblical story of Moses leading the Hebrews to the Promised Land reflected slaves' hopes for freedom for themselves.

# "Go to Sleepy, Little Baby"

A few early folk songs in the black tradition were lullabies. Among the most famous of these is a song sometimes called "Go to Sleepy, Little Baby" or "All the Pretty Little Horses." The lyric, which dates back to the days of slavery, begins as follows:

> Hush-a-bye, don't you cry,
> Go to sleepy little baby,
> When you wake, you'll have cake,
> And all the pretty little horses.

Later in the song, however, the mood abruptly changes. The singer stops describing a bright world with horses and cake and starts telling about a much grimmer scene instead:

> Way down yonder, down in the
>     meadow,
> There's a poor wee little lamby.
> The bees and the butterflies pickin'
>     at its eyes,
> The poor wee thing cried for her
>     mammy.

Some historians believe that this song is a lament sung by slave women forced to nurse and care for their masters' babies instead of their own children. The master's child is the one being sung to in the first stanza; the "lambie" referenced in the second verse is the slave's own child, left alone while the mother attends to the white baby.

Lullabies, songs sung by mothers or other caregivers to soothe babies and children, are part of the African American folk tradition.

Quoted in NIEHS Kids' Pages, "All the Pretty Little Horses (Hush-a-Bye)." http://kids.niehs.nih.gov/lyrics/prettyhorses. htm.

Spirituals were religious songs, of course, but they could have a secular, or worldly, significance as well. In particular, spirituals that referred to the afterlife often had a double meaning for many slaves. Frederick Douglass recalled singing a song called "I Am Bound for Canaan's Land" while growing up on a Maryland farm. Taken literally, "Canaan's Land" was a reference to heaven. To any whites who happened to be listening, the song simply indicated the singer's desire for a better life in the next world. But as Douglass wrote years later, "A keen observer might have detected in our repeated singing of [this spiritual] something more than a hope of reaching heaven. We meant to reach the North, and the North was our Canaan. . . . [The song] meant a speedy pilgrimage to a free state and deliverance from all the evils and dangers of slavery."[32] Singing the spiritual, therefore, was a way for slaves to express their desire to escape—and, sometimes, to communicate to one another their plans to do so as well.

## Secular Songs

Though they occupy an important place in the black folk tradition, spirituals are not by any means the only type of folk song that African Americans created. Even during the first half of the 1800s, when the popularity of spirituals was at its peak, secular songs were quite common among the slaves on Southern plantations—and among the free blacks in the North and elsewhere. These more worldly songs sometimes touched on Christian themes or biblical imagery, but they were not fundamentally about religion.

A few of these were lighthearted nonsense songs, such as "Charleston Gals," an African American folk piece that mentioned a dancing possum and a toad that unexpectedly "commenced to whistle and sing."[33] Others were satiric, often describing how slaves outwitted their masters in subtle ways. "O massa take dat new bran[d] coat/And hang it on de wall," reads the opening of one such song. "Dat darkee take dat same ole coat/And wear 'em to the ball."[34] Still others encouraged masters to treat their slaves well, praising those who provided plenty to eat and contrasting them favorably with those who did not. These songs could also

Slaves sang work songs to help pass the time or keep the pace during jobs requiring hard physical labor, such as picking cotton.

function as good-natured teasing of slaves from other farms. One song of this type asserted that the workers on another plantation were "lean an' po' [poor]. . . . Don't know whether they git 'nough ter eat or no."[35]

Many secular songs were work songs. Hard physical labor was a fact of life for most blacks of the nineteenth century and beyond. Whether they were planting crops, drilling tunnels, or laying railroad track, these African Americans could spend twelve or more hours a day performing the same motions again and again. While laborers sometimes worked alone, it was more common—and more efficient—for a group to work on the same project together. Many of these work gangs sang. "The singing together made the work go easier," write folklorists John and Alan Lomax; "[it] eased the aching backs and the aching hearts."[36]

African American laborers tended to sing work songs in the same basic way. Most often, one man in a work group would be given the responsibility of leading the song. This man would choose a tune with a tempo that matched the rhythm of the work. Pounding in stakes, for example, required a different cadence than picking cotton. The leader would often sing the verses of the song himself, while the other men took up the chorus or punctuated the lines with exclamations like "Huh!" or "Yes!" It was also common for song leaders to improvise the text—that is, to make up new words as they went along.

Black singers used a variety of songs as work songs. Occasionally, blacks used spirituals for this purpose. The famous spiritual "Michael, Row the Boat Ashore" was a good example; it was used by men who rowed boats in the waters of coastal South Carolina toward the end of the Civil War. Most work songs, indeed, were specific to the task at hand. "All I hate about linin' track," ran a song popular among men who built railroads, "these old bars gonna

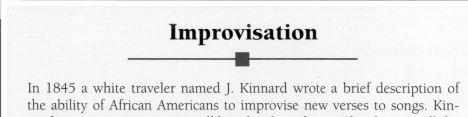

# Improvisation

In 1845 a white traveler named J. Kinnard wrote a brief description of the ability of African Americans to improvise new verses to songs. Kinnard was a passenger on a small boat heading along a Florida river; all the paddlers were black. "The negroes," Kinnard writes, "struck up a song to which they kept time with their oars. . . . There seemed to be a certain number of lines ready-manufactured, but after this stock was exhausted, lines relating to surrounding objects were extemporized [made up on the spot]. Some of these were full of rude wit, and a lucky hit always drew a thundering chorus from the rowers, and an encouraging laugh from the occupants of the stern seats."

Later in his trip, Kinnard notes another effect of the same improvisational style. "You may, in passing from Virginia to Louisiana, hear the same tune a hundred times," he writes of the songs sung by African Americans, "but seldom the same words accompanying it."

Quoted in Shane White and Graham White, *The Sounds of Slavery*. Boston: Beacon, 2005, pp. 59–60.

break my back."[37] Another song reflected the frenetic pace of picking cotton on Southern farms:

> You got to jump down, turn around,
> Pick uh bale uh cotton,
> Got to jump down, turn around
> To pick uh bale uh day.[38]

Of course, because many of the songs were composed as the song leader went along, the lyrics of most African American work songs are no longer available to us today.

## Story Songs

Other African American folk songs tell about workers and other people—some more or less true, but most exaggerated. The song, "Po' Lazarus," for instance, tells of Lazarus, a probably mythical black laborer who becomes fed up with conditions at the work camp where he is employed. According to the song, Lazarus snapped one day when he found worms in his food. He pointed a gun at the paymaster, stole the entire payroll, and disappeared into the countryside. He was soon found, however, and was shot and killed by a sheriff's deputy. While this song was not specifically a work song, it was often used in just this way. The soundtrack to the 2001 movie *O Brother, Where Art Thou?* includes an early twentieth-century recording of black prisoners singing this song as they worked.

The most famous of these story songs, however, tells of another worker: a powerfully built man named John Henry, who, according to legend, was a member of a work crew sometime during the late 1800s. Some versions of the song have the crew laying railroad tracks; others say the task was to drill a tunnel through a mountain. When his boss brings in a machine to take over the workers' jobs, John Henry insists that he is stronger and more efficient than any mechanical contraption. As one of dozens of versions of the song puts it,

> John Henry tol' his cap'n
> Dat a man was a natural man,
> An' befo' he'd let dat steam drill run him down,
> He'd fall dead wid a hammer in his han[d].[39]

The mighty John Henry wields his sledgehammer as depicted in the story song that tells of his legendary battle with a steam drill.

According to the song, John Henry and the machine's owners then hold a contest to see which can actually work the best.
Most versions of the song describe the intensity of the competition and the heavy labor that John Henry puts in to stay ahead of
the machine. "Sweat ran down like water down a hill,"[40] reports
one typical account. In the end, John Henry wins the race—but
his heart has been pushed beyond its capacity, and he falls dead.
Though some versions of the song go on to describe John Henry's
funeral and the grief of his family, others end there; certainly, the
core of the song is John Henry's victory and death.

## Stagolee

Not all the people featured in African American folk songs are
as admirable as John Henry, however. A number of black folk
songs tell of various "bad men," or violent criminals. The songs
generally treat these men as heroes, not as villains. They describe
cool, suave, and streetwise young men who go their own way
and pay little attention to the laws. "He kills without a second
thought," writes folklorist Daryl Cumber Dance, summing up the
characteristics of the typical African American folk criminal. "He
courts death constantly and does not fear dying. He loves flashy
clothes and luxury cars. He asserts his manhood through his violent physical deeds."[41] The songs about these men celebrate them
as edgy, dangerous rebels.

The most famous of these songs deals with a character nick-
named Stagolee, Stackolee, or Stagger Lee. In the songs, Stagolee
is described as a vicious, cold-blooded killer who leaves a trail of
devastation behind him. Many versions of the song describe him
shooting bartenders and raping prostitutes. But the main focus
of the songs is on Stagolee's killing of a man named Billy. In most
versions, the killing is over a dispute involving Stagolee's prized
Stetson hat, which Billy either spits into or tries to steal. The songs
about Stagolee describe this murder in gruesome detail. Typically,
they show Billy pleading for his life, but Stagolee shooting him
anyway. As one version puts it,

Billy Lyons, Billy Lyons, staggered
Through the door,
Cause Stackerlee had got him with his
Great big forty-four.[42]

36

Bluesman Mississippi John Hurt is one of many African American singers to record a version of the "Stagolee" tale.

In real life, Stagolee was probably Lee Shelton, a petty criminal in St. Louis sometimes known as "Stacker Lee." In 1895 Shelton was convicted of killing a man named Billy Lyons; the trial records indicate that a dispute over Shelton's hat did indeed lead to the murder. The songs about Stagolee, however, do not otherwise bear much resemblance to the facts of the actual Shelton case. While the real-life Shelton was caught, convicted of murder, and sentenced to jail, the fictional Stagolee is sometimes depicted as getting away with his crime. The circumstances of the murder are changed as well, including even the time period. One late twentieth-century version, collected in Philadelphia, begins, "Back in '32 when times was hard/I had a sawed-off shotgun and a crooked deck of cards."[43]

The facts of the case, though, are less important than the meaning of the song for generations of African Americans. The story of Shelton's crime struck a chord among many blacks of the period, particularly the increasing number of African Americans who had left the rural South and had begun moving to St. Louis and nearby urban areas in search of economic opportunity. Before long, songs about Stagolee had spread from Midwestern cities to black communities elsewhere as well. Like "John Henry," "Stagolee" has been sung and recorded over the years by dozens of different musicians. As one scholar puts it, "[Stagolee] is a story that black America has never tired of hearing and never stopped living out."[44]

## The Blues

Spirituals, work songs, and story songs are all important parts of African American folk music. But the folk music form most closely identified with American blacks over the years is none of these. Instead, it is the blues. The blues is a secular musical style that derives its name from so-called "blue notes," tones played at a slightly lower pitch than listeners expect. This change gives blues tunes a melancholy feel. The melancholy fits in with the texts of most blues songs, which typically speak of the troubles and sorrows of life, though often with a wryly ironic edge. The African American poet Langston Hughes sums up the character of the blues nicely when he calls them "sad funny songs—too sad to be funny and too funny to be sad."[45]

# Birth of the Blues

The great African American musician W.C. Handy was traveling through Mississippi around 1905 when he encountered a type of music that was entirely new to him. As he remembered the scene later,

> One night . . . as I nodded in the railroad station while waiting for a train, life suddenly took me by the shoulder and wakened me with a start. A lean, loose-jointed Negro had commenced plunking a guitar beside me while I slept. . . . As he played, he pressed a knife on the strings of the guitar in a manner popularized by Hawaiian guitarists who used steel bars. The effect was unforgettable. His song, too, struck me instantly.
>
> "Goin' where the Southern cross' the Dog."
>
> The singer repeated the line three times, accompanying himself on the guitar with the weirdest music I had ever heard.

Legendary musician W.C. Handy first heard the unique guitar and vocal sounds of the blues being performed by a stranger in a railroad station.

This music was the blues, and Handy's description of it was one of the first recorded. Though the music certainly sounded odd to Handy's ears, he was nevertheless drawn to its peculiar sound—and became one of the great blues musicians of his time.

Quoted in Tony Russell, *The Blues*. New York: Schirmer, 1997, p. 19.

The blues draws its musical and textual influences from other African American folk styles. The connections between the blues and spirituals, particularly the sorrow songs, are evident. There are also strong textual similarities between blues songs and many African American work songs. It was not until the early twentieth century, however, that these influences converged to form the blues as a separate musical style. Most music historians place the origin of the blues in the Mississippi Delta or in the nearby cities of Memphis, Tennessee, or New Orleans, Louisiana, although other cities and regions lay claim to being the birthplace of the style as well.

A sign near the Mississippi Delta town of Clarksdale commemorates the town's contribution to the blues.

Many blues express vague feelings of disappointment and sorrow. These songs tell about the sensation of being beaten down by circumstances, of having a life that is less than satisfying. "I believe to my soul," reads a typical example, "I'm my mama's bad luck child."[46] Other blues detail the burdens and frustrations caused by specific problems, such as poverty, lost love, imprisonment, or violence. "I don't mind being in jail, but I got to stay there so long, so long," runs a verse of a song called "Jail-House Blues," "when every friend I had is done shook hands and gone."[47]

Despite the bleakness of many blues, however, most of these songs are not simply about how grim life can be. Rather, they also express the singer's determination to continue living regardless of the obstacles. Some blues conclude by asserting that things will improve: The singer will get another love interest, find another job, or be released from prison. Even those blues that seem to wallow in self-pity usually reflect a resilience of sorts. Folklorist Daryl Cumber Dance describes the blues as "its own celebration that the blues singer can survive and give voice to his or her pain."[48] As one song puts it, "I done seen better days, but I'm puttin' up with these."[49]

Unlike earlier forms of African American folk music, such as work songs and spirituals, blues songs are often identified with specific composers. African American musician W.C. Handy, for instance, is known to be the author of the classic "St. Louis Blues"; another musician, Richard M. Jones, composed a well-known song called "Trouble in Mind." Despite the clear authorship, these songs are usually considered examples of black folk music. Different singers and instrumentalists often perform the same blues song in very different ways, substituting new lyrics, changing melodies, and altering instrumentation. Several famous versions of "St. Louis Blues," for instance, incorporate a clarinet solo that Handy did not write. In this way, even these blues songs reflect the folk process.

The folk music of black Americans is deservedly well known throughout the world today. From spirituals to work songs and from story songs to the blues, African American folk music spans an enormous variety of styles and moods. A blues singer, wounded but never quite defeated, laments a broken romance or a world that does not seem to care; a singer of a spiritual describes the peace and joy that comes with religious faith and the promise of a better life ahead. The songs of African Americans are funny and sad, hopeful and wry, upbeat and cynical. They celebrate people who are good and noble—and as songs about men such as Stagolee indicate, they also celebrate those known for their brutality. As much as any other form of African American folklore, folk music reflects the emotional range of black American life.

# Chapter Three

# Jokes, Rhymes, and More

**A**lthough folk songs and folktales are generally the best-known examples of folklore, they are far from the only ones. African American folklore encompasses a variety of other forms as well, from jump-rope rhymes to long narrative poems and from riddles to rumors, lists, and even insults. Some of these folk styles date to the earliest years of African American history. Others are strictly the product of a modern, technical age. Whatever their origins, however, each of these forms of folklore are important parts of the African American folk tradition.

## Riddles

Along with animal tales and spirituals, riddles are among the earliest known examples of African American folklore. Indeed, author and folklorist Virginia Hamilton writes that telling riddles was "one of the favorite pastimes of slaves."[50] Unfortunately, many of the riddles told by slaves in the pre–Civil War era have not survived. Folklorists of the time tended to be more interested in writing down spirituals, work songs, and stories than they were in preserving the riddles the slaves told. A few of these early riddles were collected and printed, however, and they provide an interesting glimpse into one aspect of black culture.

Most of the riddles told by slaves played on multiple meanings of words. Some of these were expressed simply and in a straightforward manner. "Something has a ear and can't hear," queried one early riddle. "What is that?"[51] The answer was an ear of corn. Another riddle asked what could fly both high and low, yet lacked wings; the solution to this one was dust. Other riddles were written in rhyme. Most of these riddles not only used wordplay but also hinted cryptically or metaphorically at the answer. "Riddle, ma riddle, as I suppose," ran an example of this type, "Hundred eyes an' never a nose."[52] The answer to the riddle was a sieve. The "eyes" were not literal eyes, of course, but rather a reference to the dozens of tiny holes in the sieve's mesh.

Riddles also feature prominently in some early African American folktales. In one, "The Riddle Tale of Freedom," a slave strikes a bargain with his master: He will tell his master a riddle, and if the master cannot solve it, the slave will have his freedom. The slave's dog, which is named Love, has just died, and so the slave takes a piece of the dog's skin and wraps it around his hand. Then he stands in front of his master, looks at the piece of skin, and gives his master the riddle: "Love I see; Love I stand./Love I holds in my right hand."[53] The master cannot guess the answer and is forced to set the slave free. Tales like these were quite popular during the era of slavery.

## Jokes

Just as African American folklore includes riddles, so too are jokes an important part of the black folk tradition. Like the riddles, African American jokes often deal with wordplay. They also rely heavily on exaggeration and absurdity for comic effect. "The shortest man I ever saw took a ladder to climb a grain of sand,"[54] runs one joke popular among African Americans in the early twentieth century. Another joke, collected during the 1920s by folklorist and author Zora Neale Hurston, has the joke teller stating a desire to be buried in a rubber coffin "so I can go bouncing through hell."[55]

Humor is an important part of African American folk stories, too. Many animal tales are in essence extended jokes. One animal story, for instance, tells of a time when Mr. Jack Sparrow was eager to pass some information on to Br'er Fox. The hungry fox pretends to be deaf, however, and insists that the sparrow come

Whether told to amuse, insult, or both, the styles of jokes enjoyed by African Americans today are rooted in the folk tradition.

closer and closer. "You better get on my back," he suggests, followed by, "Hop on my head," and finally, "Believe you better hop on my tooth. I'm deaf in one ear and can't hear out the other, but I got a little hearing in my eyetooth."[56] Br'er Fox opens his mouth invitingly, the unthinking sparrow jumps on in, and the fox, predictably enough, eats him.

As the story about Mr. Jack Sparrow indicates, many African American jokes describe foolish behavior—whether on the part of talking animals or people. Another joke collected by Hurston, for instance, describes a man who keeps extra money and food in his house. The man tells his wife that he is saving it for "Mr. Hard Time." The storyteller and the listener know perfectly well that

# Snails and Mosquitoes

Quite a few African American jokes involve animals. Several, for example, make fun of the snail and its remarkable slowness. In one, a snail is quite sick and asks her husband to go fetch the doctor. The husband agrees and begins on his way. Seven years go by, during which the poor snail suffers more and more. At last, to her delight, she hears something at the door. "Is dat you, baby, wid de doctor?" she calls to her husband, as quoted in Zora Neale Hurston's *Every Tongue Got to Confess.* But the husband shouts back, "Don't try to rush me. I ain't gone yet." A similar tale tells of a snail who takes many years to cross a road. Just as he reaches the other side, a tree falls and narrowly misses him. The snail reacts by congratulating himself on his remarkable speed.

Mosquitoes, a common pest in much of the South, also form the basis for a number of animal jokes in the African American tradition. One such joke tells of how a group of workers, tired of being attacked by mosquitoes, decided to wear suits made entirely of tin while they worked. That was not much of a barrier to the mosquitoes, however, who went home, brought back can openers, and managed to attack the men regardless. Another joke tells of a man who was driving a cart pulled by oxen through a mosquito-infested swamp. He stopped for a while to visit a friend, leaving his cart outside. When he returned, the mosquitoes had eaten the oxen and were picking their teeth with the horns!

Quoted in Zora Neale Hurston, *Every Tongue Got to Confess: Negro Folk-Tales from the Gulf States.* New York: HarperCollins, 2001, p. 255.

the name "Mr. Hard Time" simply refers to potential hard times ahead, but the man's wife, who is described as "sorta silly,"[57] does not understand this. When the husband leaves the house one day, a stranger comes by and announces that he is Mr. Hard Time. The wife cheerfully gives him the stored money and food, just as she thought she was supposed to.

African American jokes also include humorous, though barbed, insults aimed at friends or enemies. Sometimes these insults take the form of a game, known as playing or "doing the dozens," in which two or more participants try to one-up the other with progressively harsher slams, many of them obscene. These insults can be aimed directly at another player. "You're so dumb," reads one line sometimes used in the dozens today, "you tried to dial 911, but you couldn't find 11 on the phone."[58] More common, though, are insults intended for other players' relatives, usually their mothers. "Yo' mama's so ugly she went to the zoo and the gorilla paid to see her,"[59] is one typical insult of this kind.

Though playing the dozens can lead to angry feelings and even to violence, it is most often a friendly competition. "We played the Dozens for recreation like white folks play Scrabble,"[60] recalls African American activist H. Rap Brown. Indeed, playing the dozens is a way for blacks to win respect and status within their communities; African Americans who are successful with this game are much praised for their wit and quick thinking. The dozens, moreover, are growing in popularity. Once known only within heavily black neighborhoods and communities, the dozens have become a frequent feature of mainstream movies and television shows, and the phrase "Yo' mama" is familiar to millions of Americans who are white, Asian, and Latino.

## Tall Tales

Tall tales—stories that are based on exaggeration—are usually narratives, but they also have much in common with jokes. African American folk culture includes quite a few tall tales. These stories are usually, but not always, quite short, and they are designed to make readers and listeners laugh. Sometimes they include a "gotcha" element or a surprise twist at the end. In one classic tale, "Papa John" tells his son Jake that he planted an unusual turnip seed long before Jake was born. The turnip grew far bigger than any other turnip before or since, Papa John explains. When it was finally ripe, it took a year to cook, and Papa John kept eating it for years. "I sure woulda liked to [have] tasted that turnip, Papa," says Jake at the end of the story, whereupon his father responds, "You et the last piece of it for your dinner today."[61]

The turnip story is quite elaborate, but other tall tales can be much simpler. One example, collected in the Gulf States in the 1920s, tells of a family in which the mother suddenly becomes ill. Her daughter lives in another town, so the woman's son sends his

47

sister a telegram to tell her the news. The boy's father, however, takes issue with the wording of the telegram. He saddles up their horse—described in the text as the fastest horse in the world—and rides off. In a twinkling he catches up with the telegram, re-writes it, and continues to the sister's home. The moment the man leaves the house, the mother instructs the boy to start a fire for supper; but before she can finish her sentence, the horse appears in the yard, father and sister seated upon it.

African American tall tales typically draw their material from nature and ordinary life. One story, for instance, describes the

An animated storyteller can best convey the elaborate, exaggerated stories known as tall tales, which have been enjoyed and passed along by African Americans for generations.

world's largest tree. Five men tried to cut it down, the story explains, but after a week they had scarcely gotten through the outer layer of bark. Taking a break, they walked around to the other side of the tree where they met another work crew that had been chopping for six months without getting very far. Another tells of a man who went hunting and bagged several dozen animals with a single shot. His bullet cracked open a tree limb, catching the claws of several turkeys in the gap; then the bullet ricocheted, killing more animals. Meanwhile, the rifle flew out of the hunter's hands and struck and killed a deer, and the man himself "fell backwards an' smothered all dem partiges [partridges]."[62] Exaggerated jokes such as these make up a significant part of the African American folk tradition.

## Rhymes

Like riddles, tall tales, and jokes, rhyme has long been an important element of black folklore. Spirituals, blues, and work songs all incorporate rhyme into their lyrics, of course; as noted above, even some African American riddles and jokes are written in rhyme. Some black folktales include rhymes and other snippets of poetry as well. One of Joel Chandler Harris's Br'er Rabbit stories, for instance, shows the rabbit tricking Br'er Bear by having him climb into a bee's nest. "Tree stan' high, but honey mighty sweet," chants Br'er Rabbit as the bees start attacking the bear. "Watch dem bees wid stingers on der feet."[63]

Beyond their use in songs, stories, and jokes, rhymes also are part of black folklore by themselves. Many pre–Civil War observers noted that slaves often beat out elaborate rhythms by clapping their hands or tapping various parts of their bodies. While they clapped, they chanted a rhyme about a mythical slave named Juba. "Oh, 'twas Juba dis and Juba dat/Juba killed de yaller cat/To make his wife a Sunday hat,"[64] reads one version of the lyrics to this chant. The pastime became known as "patting Juba." Other clapping games were carried out to chants with names like "Hambone" and "Mary Mack."

Over the years, rhymes such as these have been particularly common among black children, who use them as nonsense chants, clapping rhymes, and counting-out verses for games. "Chick-a-my, chick-a-my Crainy Crow," begins a rhyme recorded among children

Tales of Br'er Rabbit's adventures with Br'er Bear and others often include rhyming verse within the narrative.

in Arkansas, "I went to the river to wash my toe."[65] This rhyme is often associated with a game in which one child pretends to be a witch and tries to capture the other players. Other examples of this type can either be recited or put to a sing-song melody, such as this one, collected among schoolgirls in Houston:

I wish I had a nickel
I wish I had a dime
I wish I had a boyfriend
Who kissed me all the time.[66]

Quite a few modern rhymes are connected with jumping rope, especially double Dutch, a popular activity among many black girls. Double Dutch requires a good deal of coordination; two children turn two ropes in opposite directions while other children do the actual jumping, timing their leaps carefully to avoid

Double-dutch jumpers like these girls in Brooklyn, New York, often recite fun, silly rhymes to help them keep their timing.

tripping up. Rhymes not only are fun for double-Dutch jumpers to recite while they play, but they help jumpers and rope-turners find a rhythm as well. Many rhymes also provide a structure for counting the number of jumps or determining who jumps when. "All in together, girls!" instructs one popular jump-rope rhyme. "How do you like the weather, girls? When it's your birthday, please jump in."[67] As the turners name the months, girls who were born that month start jumping.

The rhymes used by African American children typically have many variations. A New York version of a popular rhyme, used for both double Dutch and hand-clapping games, begins "Down, down, baby/Down down the rollercoaster" and ends with "Shimmy shimmy cocoapuffs/Shimmy shimmy pow."[68] Another published version of the same rhyme, this one from Texas, replaces "down the rollercoaster" with "by the waterfront" and the last two lines with "Shimmy shimmy cocoa pop/Shimmy shimmy boom."[69] The variations are testament to the widespread popularity of these rhymes among black children—and show the folk process at work.

## Toasts

Rhymes are not only the province of children, however. Adult African Americans have a long-standing tradition of toasts, or long poems that tell stories. Structurally, toasts are quite long, often a hundred lines or more, and are most often made up of rhyming couplets. Toasts typically focus on life on the streets: Drugs, violence, and crime are all frequent topics of toasts. The language of toasts is often obscene, and the descriptions of sex and violence can be quite graphic. Toasts are closely related to songs about antiheroes such as Stagolee; indeed, some folklorists consider the tale of Stagolee to be fundamentally a toast that has been set to music, rather than a song in its own right.

The specifics of toasts, however, do vary considerably. One toast tells of Kitty Barrett, an undercover police officer in New York City who specialized in drug busts. The toast describes how the narrator, a drug dealer, tried to sell Barrett drugs—and was arrested. "She slapped me and kicked me and threw me upside

# Rap Music and Toasts

The connections between toasts and rap music are not difficult to see. Structurally, both forms rely heavily on rhymes—and highly intricate rhymes at that. Both raps and toasts, moreover, are typically recited or chanted rather than sung. Nevertheless, there is a clear rhythmic beat in each style. The language of toasts and rap songs is similar in another way, too. Though there are "clean" and Christian rap songs, both raps and toasts are known for their heavy use of obscenities.

Perhaps most notably, however, the subject matter of the two forms is often the same. Both raps and toasts usually deal with impulsive young men who skirt or break the law, often by becoming involved in the drug trade. Both celebrate consumer culture in the form of fast cars, fancy clothes, and other expensive and showy items. Similarly, both raps and toasts can be extremely violent, with frequent references to guns, shootings, beatings, and murder. And both usually describe—often approvingly—the exploitation of women.

It should come as no surprise, then, that rap music is derived in part from toasts. In the 1950s several black disc jockeys in Jamaica—where toasts have long been extremely popular—began speaking or chanting toasts over the airwaves as they played records of instrumental music with a heavy beat. (They were careful to remove profanity and obvious sexual references.) Some of these entertainers called the new style "rapping," and the name stuck. The style soon spread to the United States as well and became more and more popular and well known as it developed in new directions. While other factors also helped create rap music, the most direct of all influences is the tradition of toasting.

the wall," runs a verse of one version. "Pulled her pistol and said she'd waste me if I moved a muscle at all."[70] Other toasts describe the murder of the hero, usually a criminal or drug addict. Less often, they show the central figure getting away with a crime. Some toasts involve plenty of humor; others are serious cautionary tales about the dangers of getting involved with the wrong woman, becoming addicted to drugs, or betraying a friend to the police.

While there are some written collections of toasts, the toast is at heart an oral tradition, even a performance piece. Most often, tellers recite the poems at informal gatherings in an urban setting, perhaps at a poolroom or on a street corner. Sometimes, audience members join in on the most familiar parts of the tales. Other times, the audience simply listens, especially when the speaker makes up new verses on the spot or is an especially talented performer. Like folktales and folk songs, toasts are usually changed as they pass from one person to another. "Total freedom to augment [lengthen], shorten, adapt, and improvise is one of the defining features of a toast," write the authors of a book on black folk narrative poetry. Indeed, they add, some toasts can go on "for as long as the patience, ingenuity, or stamina of the crowd lasts."[71]

## New Technologies

In modern times, African Americans have added new types of folklore to the traditional roster of stories, riddles, rhymes, and songs. Where these earlier forms of folklore were largely spread by word of mouth, however, these new styles are increasingly spread through print. More and more, contemporary African Americans are likely to circulate folklore by faxing it, e-mailing it, blogging about it, or photocopying it and distributing it to friends and family. These new technological methods have allowed African Americans to share folklore not merely with people who live and work near them, but with others who live hundreds or thousands of miles away.

Humor makes up a large portion of the folklore that modern-day African Americans pass along through these new technologies. One example is an e-mail sometimes entitled "You Went to a Black University If . . .," which plays off popular stereotypes of historically black colleges. The e-mail lists a number of wry statements about college life; if a reader thinks the statements match his or her own college experience, the e-mail concludes, it is likely that the reader attended a historically black university. The statements listed vary from version to version. One variation features statements such as "Every floor in the dorm had a barber or a beautician," "You knew exactly how many miles your car could go on 'E' [that is, empty]," and "You scheduled your classes around the Soaps."[72]

Black colleges are not the only aspect of African American culture lampooned by these lists. Other lists circulated widely among African Americans poke gentle fun at traditionally black churches, the wedding customs of urban blacks, and offices dominated by African American workers. Many black Americans also distribute lists that make fun of other groups, such as Southern whites, blonde women, or Northerners. "Don't be worried about

African Americans today keep their folklore tradition alive by using e-mail and other technology to share stories, jokes, songs, and other reflections of their culture.

not understanding what people are saying," advises one item in a list offering comical advice to Northerners who are moving to the South; "they can't understand you either."[73]

Rumors can also be passed from one person to another via photocopier or e-mail. This type of folklore tends to be much more serious than the lighthearted lists described above. Some rumors, for example, accuse certain companies of discriminating against African American consumers. In recent years, the

## "Do You Know What It Means?"

One of the most famous toasts in African American folklore is called "Do You Know What It Means?" This toast consists of a mocking set of questions delivered by a successful criminal to a younger and less powerful rival, ending in a condescending putdown. Some of the verses follow; they are quoted in the book *The Life: The Lore and Poetry of the Black Hustler.*

Do you know what it means to wear two-hundred-dollar suits and forty-dollar hats,

To drive through the streets in Fleetwood Cadillacs? . . .

Do you know what it means to give every young hustler a break,

To fill his pockets with money and his stomach with steak? . . .

Do you know what it means to have the mob call you King and the cops call you Mister,

To have the D.A. [district attorney] offer his mother and the judge put up his sister?

Do you know what it means? No, you never could know what it means, and you never will,

'Cause you're one of the chumps who pay my bill.

Quoted in Dennis Wepman, Ronald B. Newman, and Murray B. Binderman, *The Life: The Lore and Poetry of the Black Hustler.* Philadelphia: University of Pennsylvania Press, 1976, pp. 158–59.

clothing brands No Fear and Tommy Hilfiger have each been the subject of stories that have been spread in this way. Rumors such as these are often known as urban legends, a term referring to certain types of modern-day folklore. Urban legends move quickly from one person to the next, usually sound believable, and are frequently supported by what seem to be first-person accounts or other evidence. However, most urban legends are not accurate, and the rumors about No Fear and Tommy Hilfiger are entirely unfounded.

Not all such rumors are, however. In 2006, for instance, an e-mail charged that some stores in the CVS drugstore chain put electronic antitheft tags on hair care products designed to be sold to African Americans—but not on equivalent products meant for other ethnic groups. Some observers dismissed this story as yet another inaccurate urban legend involving race. But the CVS rumor turned out to have a factual basis. When reporters for television stations in Missouri and South Carolina investigated the tale, they found that some of the chain's stores were doing exactly what the e-mail claimed.

The government is a common theme of urban legends that have particular appeal to black Americans. One of these stories, for example, asserts that Social Security numbers have a hidden code identifying the holder's race. "Rumor has it some companies are looking at potential employee's SS#s to discriminate,"[74] the e-mail notes. This rumor is untrue; the assignment of Social Security numbers, in fact, has nothing to do with race. Another e-mail widely circulated among African Americans says that all blacks are entitled to a tax refund as reparations, or payback, for slavery. "Request an application for yourself, husband, wife, sister, brother, father, mother, etc." reads one version of this e-mail. "God Bless You All and please check this out!!!!!!!!"[75] Although as of 2008 the federal government has not authorized any such tax credit, hopeful African Americans continue to pass this and similar urban legends on to their friends and families.

While folklorists have traditionally focused most of their energies on the study of folk songs and folk stories, the rich variety of rhymes, riddles, and even e-mails suggests the strength of the folk process in African American culture. Jump-rope rhymes show how folklore is spread among children; rumors point to how it can be passed on in a modern, technological age. Toasts are a window into a crueler, meaner world than the one described in most black folk stories and many, though certainly not all, black folk songs. The growing popularity of African American traditions, such as the dozens, demonstrates the impact of black culture on American society as a whole. The riddles, rhymes, toasts, and rumors of the black tradition add immeasurably to our knowledge and understanding of African American folklore.

## Chapter Four

# Roots and Influences

Tracing the origins of folklore is complicated. Usually, folklorists can do little more than make an educated guess about the roots of a given story or song. They do that primarily by looking for similarities in folklore types and styles among cultures. When two cultures come into contact with one another, whether for the purposes of trade, exploration, or warfare, they often pick up aspects of each other's folklore. Traveling merchants bring back the stories and songs of other peoples; conquerors incorporate into their own traditions the riddles and tales of those they have defeated. If two cultures share a set of stories or song lyrics, that may be evidence that one of these cultures has influenced the other's folklore.

But that is scarcely a guarantee. For one thing, it can be extremely difficult to tell which culture influenced the other—or whether a third culture originated the song or story and influenced the other two. Written records seldom go back more than a century or two, not long enough to make much of a determination about the original source. For another, very different cultures often have strikingly similar folklore despite having had virtually no contact whatsoever. Variations of the Cinderella tale, for instance, are found among peoples across the globe.

Cultures from around the world share many folktales rooted in the same basic premise, such as the story of Cinderella.

Even if two cultures share stories or riddles that are much alike, then, it does not follow that one culture influenced the other.

Nonetheless, there are good reasons to suspect that African American folklore draws at least in part on two identifiable sources. One is the various folk traditions of the peoples of West Africa. These include the Yoruba of present-day Nigeria, the Wolof of Senegal, the Ewe of Ghana and Benin, and the Mbundu of Angola, among many other disparate groups. The other is the folklore of northwestern Europe, including Germany, Holland, and France, but even more notably England, Scotland, and Ireland. The evidence suggests that these two traditions came together on North American soil to form a distinctively African American body of folklore: part African, part European, and entirely unique.

## Early Years

African American history begins with the advent of the slave trade across the Atlantic Ocean. This brutal form of commerce began in the early 1500s, with the first slaves going to tropical regions such as Brazil and the Caribbean. By the early 1600s, slaves were being brought to North America as well. Slaves were cheap labor, which was needed in abundance on New World plantations where crops such as sugar and rice were grown. And since virtually all Europeans of the time considered black Africans to be almost subhuman, there seemed to be no ethical problems with enslaving people and bringing them thousands of miles from their homes.

Thrust into a new and brutal world in America, some slaves found solace in sharing the familiar folk traditions of their native Africa.

Nor did obtaining African slaves prove difficult. European traders simply boarded a ship, sailed to the West African coastline, and kidnapped or traded for the slaves they needed. They chained their prisoners in crowded, filthy conditions below the decks of their ships and brought them to the New World. Many of the slaves did not survive the voyage. Those who did were taken off the ships in South Carolina, Massachusetts, or Virginia, to find themselves trapped in a new and entirely unfamiliar land. They did not know the language of their white captors; they had been torn permanently from friends and families; they had no hope of ever seeing their homes again. These new Americans were disoriented, terrified, and heartsick.

Under these circumstances, it makes sense that the newly arrived slaves of the 1600s and 1700s clung as much as they could to their own cultural traditions—including their folklore. In a harsh and brutal world where everything familiar had vanished, the stories and songs of Africa could serve as pleasant reminders of the way life had once been. As one folklorist puts it, "The elements of storytelling were included in the only 'baggage' [the slaves] could carry with them: their traditional styles [and] their ways of performing and celebrating."[76] These cultural traditions gave comfort and strength to the new Americans—and they were reinforced by the constant arrival of more and more Africans as the slave trade continued.

## Folktales

Indeed, there are many strong connections between West African traditions and various elements of African American folklore. One of the clearest relationships involves folk stories. A number of folktales collected among African Americans are strikingly similar to tales widely told in parts of Africa. A story known in the United States as "A Strange Way to Sleep" is an excellent example. In this tale, a rabbit observes a turkey taking a nap with its head under its wing. Since the rabbit cannot see the turkey's head, he assumes that the turkey has taken its head off before going to bed. The rabbit then returns to his home and tells his wife that he plans to remove his own head, too. "It is less trouble to sleep without a head,"[77] he explains—and his wife looks on in horror as he severs his head with an axe.

# Elephant and Whale

Another example of a tale that is widespread in both Africa and among African Americans is a story called "The Tug-of-War Between Elephant and Whale." The typical American telling of this tale describes how a rabbit played a joke on these two large animals. First, the rabbit enlists an elephant to help pull a cow out of the mud. The cow does not actually exist, but the elephant does not know that. After tying one end of a long rope around the elephant's neck, the rabbit takes the other end of the rope to a whale and asks for the same favor. The result is that the two large animals spend most of the day tugging to get the "cow" out of the mud; in reality, of course, they are pulling against each other.

A variation of this tale, also found in the United States, has a small animal claim that a much larger animal cannot pull him out of the water. One of the Uncle Remus stories, for example, describes this situation with Br'er Terrapin, a kind of turtle, and the more powerful Br'er Bear. Br'er Terrapin is tied to a rope and gets into the water; but before Br'er Bear starts pulling, the turtle slips loose and reattaches the rope to some underwater roots. Then he sits back and watches while Br'er Bear strains unsuccessfully to move the rope.

Other versions of both these stories are common in Africa. There are, to be sure, a few differences between the African tales and their American counterparts. African legends usually replace the trickster rabbit or turtle with Anansi the spider, who fills roughly the same role among many West African peoples. One African version of these stories, moreover, functions as a *parce que* tale, it explains why there are high and low tides today. For the most part, however, examples of these tales from the two continents deal with similar themes and plotlines. The stories have also been recorded among blacks in the Caribbean and Brazil—demonstrating how this particular folk story has caught hold among Africans and their descendants everywhere.

Stories of this type are likewise common in the African tradition. One example tells of a rooster that hides his own head under a wing. Like the rabbit in the American story, a leopard sees the rooster and wonders aloud why the head is missing. Without raising his head, the rooster explains that he cut it off and sent it out to gather food. The dim-witted leopard thinks this sounds like a good idea, so he asks a group of people to cut off his own head. The consequences are clear to the story's audience, and to the leopard's wife as well, but not to the leopard. "The people came and laid him down," one version of the story explains, "and one [person] took an axe and cut off his head at the neck, and he died immediately."[78]

The two tales are not identical, of course. In the African version, the rooster deliberately tricks the leopard, but the American account describes a simple misunderstanding. The African story is more elaborate, too, and goes on to explain that modern-day leopards chase roosters because they are angry about the trickery described in the tale—a detail absent in the American version. And, of course, the animals featured in the narrative are not the same. But these changes are relatively small compared to the many resemblances between the two stories. Though no one knows for sure, it is probable that a version of the African tale arrived in North America with some of the slaves. Once in the New World, the story was told and retold, with several details changing as it passed from one person to the next. The basic structure of the plot, however, remained the same.

There are many thematic connections between African stories and the folktales of African Americans, too. While trickster tales are common in cultures throughout the world, for instance, they are particularly prominent in the folklore of both West Africans and black Americans. Again, there are differences between the tales of these two cultures. African trickster tales frequently revolve around a spider, often named Anansi, while their American counterparts most often focus on the playful Br'er Rabbit. Even here, though, some similarities are evident. There are African tales about trickster rabbits, such as "All the Small Animals," in which Rabbit is described as outwitting Lion. And some trickster tales about spiders have been noted among African Americans over the years as well, including a few from Georgia and the Carolinas about a spider whose name has been anglicized, or changed, to "Ann Nancy."

Another parallel between African and African American folktales involves language. Quite a few black American folktales include what seem to be nonsense words. Most often, these appear in chants or songs within the text. A version of the African American folktale "A Wolf and Little Daughter," for example, has the character Little Daughter sing the words "Tray-bla, tray-bla, tray-bla, cum qua, kimo."[79] Some phrases of this kind may well be purely nonsensical, but many folklorists argue that others are remnants of sentences and songs in various African languages, changed through the folk process to a point where they no longer have a recognizable meaning.

## Songs and Music

The connections between African folklore and the folk traditions of North American blacks are perhaps even more evident in songs than in stories. Historians and folklorists have traced a great many features of African American music back to West African roots. African folk music, for instance, relies heavily on call-and-response, in which a leader sings or chants a solo line and is answered by a chorus. Call-and-response is likewise quite common in black American work songs, and it can be an important element in spirituals as well. "The leading singer starts the words of each verse, often improvising," a collector of spirituals wrote in 1867, "and the others, who 'base' him, as it is called, strike in with the refrain."[80]

Another example involves the use of rhythm. West African folk music is based in large part on drumming. Most traditional music of the region features strong, driving rhythms, often of great complexity, played on various kinds of percussion instruments. Slaves in early America were usually forbidden to own or make drums, since slaveowners feared that they might incite rebellion by using drums to send coded messages from one plantation to another. However, the slaves could—and did—engage in hand-clapping games and other activities that incorporated the intricate rhythms of West Africa. "The young, brown-skinned woman [patted] out a beat on the ground with her feet," an observer wrote about a slave in 1850, "at the same time beating out a rhythm on her chest and legs with her hands. People crowded closer, caught by the quiet, distinct, funky sound."[81]

The singing styles of American blacks also reflect styles popular in West Africa. During the Civil War, for example, folk song collector Lucy McKim noted that African American singing often included "slides from one note to another" and "odd turns made in the throat."[82] These effects are common in African folk songs, but they sounded highly unusual to the ears of McKim, who had never heard them used in the European musical tradition familiar to white Americans of the time. Today, African-style slides and turns live on not only in black spirituals but in other musical forms as well, including jazz, gospel, rock, and the blues—each heavily influenced by black folk culture.

One musical tradition in the nineteenth-century South was particularly closely connected with African folk practices. This was the ring shout, which combined movements and music into a ritual with religious meaning. A shout could last two or three hours, and it often had a hypnotic effect on the participants. According to an 1867 eyewitness account, participants in a shout "begin first walking and, by and by, shuffling around, one after another, in a ring. . . . Sometimes they dance silently . . . and sometimes the song itself is also sung by the dancers. But more frequently a band, composed of some of the best singers, stand at the side of the room . . . singing the body of the song and clapping their hands together or on their knees."[83]

White observers of the time found the shout so different from their own customs that they automatically assumed an African origin for it, although they knew little or nothing about the music or cultures of West Africa. Today, further research into African traditions has demonstrated that this theory is substantially correct. "The call-and-response singing," writes a modern commentator, "the [multiple rhythms] of the . . . hands and feet, the swaying and hitching shuffle of the shouters, all derive from African forms."[84] It is even possible that the name *shout* stems from an Arabic word commonly used in West Africa. In any case, the shout is an unusually clear example of a black American custom with African roots.

## Loss of Culture

But although some African traditions continued to flourish in North America, the realities of North American slave life made it difficult for customs and folklore to survive intact. One reason involved geography. Until about 1800, the great majority of slaves lived in rela-

# Native American Roots

—■—

The first inhabitants of the southeastern United States were various Native American groups, such as the Cherokee, the Creek, and the Seminole. Over time these peoples were gradually pushed westward and into the rugged mountain areas by the growing number of white settlers. For many years, however, groups such as the Cherokee lived near white people and their slaves. Some, indeed, owned African American slaves themselves. Even those who did not often had plenty of contact with the slaves of the Southeast.

As a result, African American folklore has some Native American roots and influences. Exactly how much is a matter of dispute. Some Cherokee tales, for example, are strikingly similar to the African American folk stories about Br'er Rabbit. Like their counterparts from the black tradition, these stories describe the adventures of a prankster rabbit that uses his wits and guile to outsmart other animals. Some of the stories even revolve around the same basic tricks. Certainly, some of these tales were collected from the Cherokee even before Joel Chandler Harris set the Br'er Rabbit tales down in book form. This has led some researchers to suggest that black Americans derived some of their material directly from the lore of the Cherokee and other Indian groups. The extent of the influence, however, is difficult to determine, and it is of course possible that the stories flowed from the slaves to the Native Americans instead—or even that the similarities are wholly coincidental.

tive isolation from one another. While there were some large plantations with dozens or hundreds of slaves during this period, few masters of the time owned more than ten slaves; many had fewer than five. Most slaves rarely traveled far from their homes, and only a small number lived in urban areas. Free blacks of the period were likewise widely scattered. As a result, the typical African American of the time had relatively little contact with other blacks—and relatively little opportunity, therefore, to share riddles, folktales, and songs they remembered from Africa.

That was particularly true because slaves were rarely kept together with others from their own culture or ethnicity. The eight or ten slaves living on a typical farm might include representatives of three or four different peoples from several regions of Africa. These slaves did not necessarily share a common body of folklore. For that matter, they often spoke different languages. Under these circumstances, it could be difficult for even highly motivated slaves to preserve their folk traditions. All too often, there was no opportunity to share tales or songs with someone else who knew them.

Language represented a problem in another way, too. While the first blacks in North America spoke African languages, these languages were soon replaced by English. The shift in language caused the loss of countless song lyrics, stories, and riddles. Most puns, for example, could not have survived the transition from an African language to English. Puns rely for their humor on words that sound alike, and similar-sounding African words generally do not have similar-sounding English translations. Other folklore forms could be translated, but they suffered in the process. Song lyrics lost their rhythm; poems lost their rhymes. The shift to English made it difficult to keep these aspects of African folklore alive.

## European Influences

To fill the gap, American blacks adopted a number of folk traditions from their European masters. While there were strong racial and social divides between blacks and whites, most colonial blacks lived and worked in close proximity to white people. A slave woman assigned to serve dinner to a farm family, for instance, would often overhear stories of European origin being told around the table. Similarly, a slave man might hear songs sung by his master while the two labored together to repair a fence or to begin the spring planting. These stories, songs, and other bits and pieces of folklore stemmed largely from the British Isles, where the majority of the colonists had their roots. Many of these songs and narratives became common among African Americans as well.

One example of the European connection to black American folklore involves a story often called "Tailypo" or "The Peculiar Such Thing." As told in the African American tradition, the narrative tells of a man awakened one night by a mysterious voice that says, "Tailypo, tailypo. Give me back my tailypo." The man struggles to see who—or what—is speaking, but he can make out nothing in the darkness. Nor does he have any idea what a tailypo is. As the voice comes closer and closer, the man becomes more and more alarmed. "I hasn't got it!" he insists, but the creature shouts, "Yes you has!"[85] The creature then jumps on the man and tears him to bits. While there are certainly many tales of monsters in the African tradition, the details of this particular story make it much more reminiscent of narratives from England and elsewhere in Europe.

Folk music provides another example of European influences on African American folklore. White Americans brought traditional

Slaves are depicted gathered for a prayer meeting engaged in lively dance and songs, the melodies of which were likely based on traditional European music.

# White Folklore

As this chapter makes clear, European folklore has had an important influence on the folklore of African Americans. At the same time, black American folk traditions have helped shape the folklore of white Americans, too. This process is probably most evident in music. Various black folk styles over the years have made their way into formerly European traditions such as country music, Western swing, and "white spirituals"—religious songs sung largely by frontier families with roots in the British Isles. As John and Alan Lomax write in their book *Best Loved American Folk Songs,* "The story of the development of the white spiritual since the early part of the nineteenth century . . . is one of steady progress toward the most favored Negro song structure—simplicity of language, feeling more important than meaning in the lines, much repetition, choruses coming every four lines, choruses that wander from song to song." Instruments such as the banjo, common in musical forms like bluegrass, were brought to the United States by Africans as well.

Today, the influence of black folk styles is more evident than ever in mainstream American music. The rhythms and harmonies of modern-day pop music are derived in part from jazz and the blues; rap music, based in turn on older forms of black folklore such as toasts, is popular well beyond the black community. Even classically oriented white composers have incorporated elements of spirituals, jazz, and other traditional African American materials into their works. Over time, black American music has had enormous influence on the music of white Americans.

John and Alan Lomax, *Best Loved American Folk Songs.* New York: Grosset and Dunlap, 1947, p. 332.

songs and dance tunes with them from Europe. They sang ballads while they worked; they picked up fiddles at night and played jigs and reels. On Sundays, they sang hymns and other religious music that followed standard European rules of melody, harmony, and rhythm. Except on the largest plantations, blacks could scarcely avoid hearing these examples of European-based music. As twentieth-century folklorists John and Alan Lomax put it, "Many phrases and lines, many melodic ideas were learned by the Negroes from the whites;

many songs, sung by the Negroes as spirituals, were adaptations of white revival [that is, religious] songs."[86]

As a result, the melodies of spirituals and other black folk songs often had much more in common with traditional music of white Americans than with the music of Africa. That, of course, was not at all clear to the white song collectors of the nineteenth century, who focused their attentions on the differences between European music and the music of the blacks. Still, if typical Africans of the time had heard the music of black North Americans, they would almost surely have pointed to the many important differences in melody, rhythm, and instrumentation between that music and their own—and argued that African American music was not African at all, but rather highly "European."

## Christian Ideas

European religion also had a strong influence on African American folklore. Though the first Africans to arrive in North America typically practiced African tribal religions, most slaves had adopted Christianity before the 1800s. Many commentators, then and now, have pointed out that Christianity as practiced by African Americans of the time shared important features with African spiritual traditions. These include audience participation in sermons, an emphasis on emotion during worship, and the establishment of a personal relationship with God and Jesus. And, of course, the singing of American blacks was in part derived from the musical styles of Africa.

Nonetheless, the effect of Christianity on black American folklore was great. The texts of African American spirituals, after all, drew on stories from the Bible, not on tales of West African gods and spirits. Many folktales also reflected biblical themes. One story, collected in the 1920s, tells of a stingy man who dies and tries to enter heaven. The man tells Peter and John, two of Jesus' followers who are acting as gatekeepers, that he has done two good things during his life. Once, he explains, he gave two cents to a child who had lost a nickel. The other time, he gave three cents to another child who had also lost a nickel. "Is you goin' let him in, Peter?" asks John. Peter shakes his head. "Give him his damn nickel back," he says, "and let him gwan [go on] to hell."[87] Though the dialect used in this telling of the story is distinctively African American, the imagery of this story is derived from European ideas of heaven and hell.

A white woman is depicted reading the Bible to slaves, who widely adopted Christianity while maintaining some traditional African elements in their worship.

It is clear, then, that African American folklore is strongly rooted in two powerful folk traditions. In some cases, such as vocal styles, the role of rhythm in folk music, or folktales that feature tricksters, the African impact seems especially evident. In others, such as the prevalence of Christian imagery and the melodic and harmonic structure of many black folk songs, the European influence appears predominant. The truth is, however, that African American folklore is not truly African, nor precisely European. It is, instead, something original and new: a blend of images and styles, a reworking of old and familiar ideas in fresh and vital ways. This distinctive African American folklore tradition has added depth, strength, and life to American culture.

## Chapter Five

# Shaping the Black Experience

Folklore is passed from one person to another, and from one generation to the next, for a variety of reasons. Perhaps the most straightforward of these reasons is that folklore is entertaining. Children eagerly seek out the latest knock-knock jokes or ghost stories to pass on to their friends. People read books of fairy tales and attend performances of folk music. Indeed, folklore that does not engage people does not last. No one wants to hear a dull story, or a joke with a punch line that makes no sense. Folklore, in this context, is a creative outlet for those who tell stories, sing songs, or recite rhymes and chants—and an appealing way to spend time for those who form the audience for the tellers.

But folklore is more than mere entertainment. The folklore of a culture often springs directly from the heart of its people. The types of tales people tell, the kinds of songs they sing, the varieties of poems they recite, all grow out of the hopes, dreams, and sorrows of the group. Tales that seem to speak to the group's history or current situation have a better chance of lasting than tales that do not. For better or for worse, the folklore of a given culture is tightly bound to the culture itself. In some sense, then, people create the songs and jokes they do because those pieces of their folk tradition speak to something deep inside them.

Since folklore is so tightly connected to culture, moreover, it can become a marker of ethnic, regional, or racial identity. Most people see themselves as belonging to one or more groups—college students, say, or fans of a given sports team, or people who live in a certain town or neighborhood. Teenagers who dress in black or wear their hair in a mullet are making statements about the group with which they identify. Speaking with an accent or using specific slang terms can do the same thing. Similarly, those who pass on the songs and stories of their culture do so in part to affirm that they belong to that culture—and often because they wish others to see them that way, too.

The connections between folklore and culture are as true for African Americans as they are for any other group. Whether humorous or sorrowful, whether in story or in song, African American folklore has always reflected the black experience in the United States. Black folklore, in truth, speaks to the core of what it means to be African American. Indeed, folklore is in many ways at the heart of black culture. By cherishing and sharing folk songs, folk stories, and folk riddles, blacks over the years have created and cemented a group identity. In ways both great and small, folklore has helped African Americans to build a culture and to survive as a people.

## Br'er Rabbit

The links between African American folklore and African American culture and history are easy to find. One clear example has to do with the popular folk stories about Br'er Rabbit. On the surface, these tales are innocent stories about animals. But Br'er Rabbit's adventures also spoke to pre–Civil War slaves on a deeper level. The rabbit's never-ending battle with his enemies reflects the struggle between the relatively powerless slaves and the white masters who held all the weapons. As Virginia Hamilton writes, "The early generations of African American [story]tellers during slavery knew that the little rabbit they saw hopping along was small and helpless. . . . They were helpless as well, and they began to identify the rabbit's lowly status with their own."[88]

The fact that the plucky little rabbit generally wound up the victor in the Br'er Rabbit tales was also important in making these

# Br'er Rabbit and Violence

While Br'er Rabbit usually settles for humiliating his enemies, some of the Br'er Rabbit tales end with the rabbit physically injuring the other animals. In one tale, for instance, he drops a brick on Br'er Fox's head; in another, he pours scalding water onto Br'er Wolf. From one perspective, these stories do not reflect slave life at all. Despite a handful of well-publicized slave rebellions over time, it was extremely rare for slaves to respond with violence toward whites.

Still, many slaves came close to it. One former slave described his reaction when his mistress's daughter slapped him. "I hit at her with my fist and with all the force I had," he later recalled. "I was just about ready to . . . choke the life out of her when ol' Missy [the girl's mother] happened in." Like the stories that close with the fox or the wolf deeply embarrassed and ashamed, then, the Br'er Rabbit folk stories that include violence also most likely reflect the wishes of many a plantation slave—though hidden in the form of an innocent animal story.

Quoted in Julius Lester, *To Be a Slave*. New York: Dial, 1968, pp. 127–28.

Although most tales depict Br'er Rabbit using his wiles to defeat his foes, he is occasionally driven to violence.

stories popular. While slaves were under the control of their masters, a clever slave could usually find a way of avoiding work. Some slaves rested whenever they knew they were not being watched. Others successfully pretended to be ill. Still others played dumb, pretending not to understand directions or never actually carrying them out. "Their way of managing not to do [an assigned task] was very ingenious," wrote a Georgia plantation owner. "They always were perfectly good-tempered, and received my orders with, 'Dat's so, missus; just as missus says,' and then somehow or other left the thing undone."[89]

By avoiding work for a day or an hour, the slaves were not striking a mortal blow against the slave system. But though these were only small victories, they were undeniably victories. First, of course, they brought the slaves some needed rest. Second, and perhaps more important, they gave the slaves the satisfaction of having fooled their masters, however briefly, and the realization that they could at least sometimes be in control of their own fates. The victories of the fictional Br'er Rabbit against the much more powerful Br'er Fox and Br'er Wolf reflected the minor victories of the slaves and afforded them an extra measure of delight at the rabbit's cleverness and trickery.

## Humiliation and Anger

The ways in which Br'er Rabbit emerges victorious also speak to the reality of slave life. Most often, Br'er Rabbit publicly humiliates those who wish him harm. In one tale, for instance, Br'er Rabbit wants to ride on Br'er Fox's back, and he talks the fox into agreeing. Br'er Rabbit then guides the unsuspecting fox to the house of a recurring human character, Miz Meadows. He dismounts, ties Br'er Fox to a tree, and explains that Br'er Fox has been his family's personal riding horse for thirty years. Br'er Fox is deeply ashamed, but Miz Meadows and her daughters "laughed so hard and so long," according to Julius Lester's version of the tale, "they liked to broke out of their underclothes."[90]

The embarrassment of Br'er Fox in this tale, and others like it, would certainly have appealed to the slaves. Many former slaves spoke and wrote of their angry feelings toward their masters—feelings usually hidden from view in the presence of whites. Their complaints ranged from the severity of punishment to the lack of adequate food and clothing. "At times they would give us enough to eat," recalled a slave from Georgia. "At times they wouldn't—just 'cording to how they feeling when they dishing out the grub."[91] Br'er Rabbit's humiliation of Br'er Fox was an indication of what slaves would have done to their masters—if they only had the chance.

This is not to say that the Br'er Rabbit tales are "really" about the slaves, or that the stories were written specifically to model and reflect the world of the first American blacks. The existence

Tales in which Br'er Fox is outsmarted by the cunning Br'er Rabbit can be seen as allegories depicting a slave's desire to humiliate his master.

of stories in which Br'er Rabbit gets a punishment of some sort demonstrates that not all these tales show the world as the slaves wished it to be. Similarly, it is not clear that all—or even most—blacks who told the Br'er Rabbit stories saw them as metaphors for the condition of black Americans. Still, whether blacks who told the stories were conscious of it or not, the adventures of Br'er Rabbit *did* speak to the African American experience—and that connection boosted the popularity of the stories over the years.

## Other Folk Stories

The Br'er Rabbit stories, of course, are not the only folktales that reflect African American culture and history. The John tales, which deal with the trials and tribulations of a slave, stem even more clearly from the realities of black life. Many blacks dreamed of winning their own freedom or of humiliating their own masters as the fictional John sometimes did. Slaves could also relate to the punishments John suffered, usually unfairly, at the hands of his master. And they understood perfectly John's complaints about being overworked, as described in a prayer from one of these tales: "Old Massa works me so hard, and doesn't give me time to rest. So come, Lord, with peace in one hand and pardon in the other, and take me away from this sin-sorrowing world. I'm tired and I want to go home."[92]

Tales of the supernatural provide a different kind of example. These stories spring directly from the spiritual beliefs of early African Americans. During the slavery era and often beyond, African American religious traditions typically accepted the existence of the devil and other evil spirits. For many black storytellers and audiences over the years, stories about evil beings have not simply been a fun way to cause shivers. Rather, they have been cautionary tales of how to act when encountering the spirit world. These stories have survived partly because they are good stories, but also because they describe an important part of the African American worldview.

The people who appear in post–Civil War African American folktales and jokes also are drawn from black culture. Ever since slavery, for instance, many black Americans have relied heavily on churches for spiritual and social support. For years, the preacher was at the center of black community life; even today, that remains true in many places. It is not surprising, then, that many jokes and folktales in collections today refer to preachers. In her anthology of 1920s folklore, for example, Zora Neale Hurston includes a twenty-four page section of preacher tales. Other common figures in black folklore include salesmen, hunters, and industrial workers, all of them figures familiar to blacks of the time. Though John Henry probably did not exist, his experiences as a laborer would have been recognizable to thousands of black men over the years who did the same sort of hard, tedious work.

## Spirituals and the Blues

Examples from black folk music also show the connection of folklore to black culture and history. Sorrow songs reflect the sadness with which blacks often viewed the world during slavery times. Pleas to Jesus were frequent and impassioned in black singing of the era; the realities of black existence seemed sometimes so overwhelming that only an appeal to God would do. "De harder yo' crosses, de brighter yo' crown,"[93] runs a verse of a well-known spiritual; the singer is expressing hope that the people with the greatest suffering on earth will have the greatest reward in heaven. Since enslaved blacks suffered more "crosses" than almost any other group in American history, it is not difficult to see how songs such as this reflected the black experience.

In the same way, spirituals are full of songs about Moses and the Exodus of the Israelites from Egypt—an obvious reference to the fact that like the Israelites before them, the majority of African Americans before 1865 were enslaved. Singing about the Exodus gave voice to the slaves' longing for a Moses and a Promised Land of their own. Like the songs that urged Jesus to intervene, the songs about Moses provided hope, however small, in the face of great sorrow. The same was true of songs that referred to other Hebrew prophets. "Didn't my Lord deliver [that is, save] Daniel?" queried one famous spiritual text. "Then why not every man?"[94]

Just as spirituals grew out of slavery, so too did the reality of black life in the early 1900s spark a folklore style of its own: the blues. Blacks of the time were oppressed in many different areas of life. They were generally poorer and less educated than whites; they were more likely to be unemployed; and whether through laws or through threats of violence, they were often kept from

# Festivals

◼

Closely related to folklore are festivals of various kinds. African Americans developed several major festivals during the eighteenth and nineteenth centuries. One of these, known variously as "Johnkannaus," "John Canoe," and "John Koonering," was an end-of-the-year extravaganza popular among slaves on Southern plantations. Part music, part drama, and part pageantry, the Johnkannaus celebration involved dancing, costumes, and raucous behavior. This festival was scheduled just after the Christmas celebration, the one time of year when slaves typically were given very little work to do, and the slaves took full advantage of the opportunity. Typically, two or three people dressed in elaborate costumes while others played musical instruments, sang, or danced in a way described by one observer as "a combination of bodily contortions, flings, kicks, gyrations, and antics of every imaginable description."

Similar festivals took place elsewhere and at other times of the year. Albany, New York, was known for its celebration of Pinkster Day, held each spring near the Christian holy day of Pentecost. New Orleans was the site of elaborate festivals around the time of Mardi Gras, or Shrove Tuesday, which usually falls in February. During these celebrations, blacks dressed up in fancy costumes and rode on floats through the streets of the city. All these festivals relied in part on folk arts. Like folk songs and folktales, these celebrations served to bring African Americans together and helped to create a strong and lasting culture.

Quoted in Daryl Cumber Dance, *From My People: 400 Years of African American Folklore*. New York: W.W. Norton, 2002, p. 183.

African American men participate in Mardi Gras festivities, which are rooted in folk traditions.

voting. Segregation, or the enforced separation of the races, was the law almost everywhere in the South—and sometimes beyond. Denied access to education, jobs, and the political process, blacks of the time usually lived in poverty and saw little hope of much change. The blues were a reflection of the conditions under which many African Americans lived.

## Creating and Telling Tales

African American folklore does not simply reflect black culture and history, however. On the contrary, folklore has often helped to draw African Americans together and give them a sense of unity. This is especially visible in the ways that folklore is created and passed on within African American society. The folk process, in general, is a communal one, in which different people add, subtract, and alter material in order to create a more or less standard version of a particular story or song. Many blues songs of the early twentieth century, in particular, bear the signs of having been traded back and forth from one singer to another. They belong to no single musician or group; instead, they are the collective property of blues musicians everywhere.

Earlier songs and stories also show group dynamics at work in the folk process. During the Civil War, a white army officer asked a black man how the slaves created songs. "Dey make 'em, sah," the African American responded, and then gave an example: "My master call me up, and order me a short peck of corn [that is, low rations] and a hundred lash [a severe whipping]. My friends see it, and is sorry for me. When dey come to de praise meeting dat night dey sing about it. Some's very good singers and know how; and dey work it in—work it in, you know, till they get it right; and dat's de way."[95] As this source makes clear, the creation of this song was the work of not just one or two people; rather, it was the collaborative effort of men and women who valued music and used song as a way to show sympathy for a troubled companion.

The simple act of telling folktales can also help to develop a sense of togetherness. Most reports indicate that storytelling was a serious business among many blacks during the 1800s. "The telling of black folktales," writes Julius Lester, "was a social event bringing together adults and children."[96] Within African American culture, moreover, storytelling has often been a way to achieve notice and praise. "A good

African American folklore remains vibrant today because of the work of storytellers like Eric Strong, who demonstrates the tradition in a presentation to students during Black History Month.

teller is almost never interrupted,"[97] write the authors of a book about African American folk poetry. The emphasis that blacks put on good storytelling, too, tends to increase the importance of folklore in African American society. By becoming adept at reciting poetry and telling stories, African Americans can carve an identity for themselves within their communities.

Telling certain kinds of folklore also carries cultural significance. The John stories are a good example. These stories and the Br'er Rabbit stories have similar themes, but while the animal stories seem innocent on the surface, the John tales are very clearly about slaves and their masters. During slavery, it was perfectly acceptable for a white person to hear a story about Br'er Rabbit. But the John stories were far more inflammatory. As a result, Daryl Cumber Dance points out, these tales

# Children and Folktales

Today folktales are generally believed to appeal mainly to children. Fairy tales such as Cinderella and Snow White have been made into G-rated movies. Collections of traditional stories are easiest to find in the children's rooms of libraries. In the same way, ghost stories are most often considered suitable for children to tell one another around a campfire or at a sleepover party. It is not that adults never tell or read these stories today, but the modern mindset is that these stories are primarily intended for children.

That was definitely not the case, however, among African Americans during the nineteenth century. "Traditionally, tales were told by adults to adults," writes Julius Lester in the introduction to his book *The Tales of Uncle Remus.* "If the children were quiet, they might be allowed to listen." From a cultural perspective, that makes some sense. The stories belonged to the adults; they were a way in which adult African Americans made sense of their world. Moreover, many traditional folktales include subject matter that is graphic or disturbing. The stories of Annie Christmas and John Henry end with the deaths of the main characters. Violence in folktales is common, and some stories include obvious sexual themes and occasional obscenities. In these ways, traditional folktales are actually more appropriate for adults than for children.

Julius Lester, *The Tales of Uncle Remus.* New York: Dial, 1987, p. xv.

"had to remain underground, carefully concealed among the slaves."[98] Telling the John tales, even secretly, was an act of defiance—and served to draw African Americans closer together as they made sure to keep these stories a secret from the outside world.

Even the joking e-mails and rumors that bounce between the desks of modern African Americans can help to build a sense of unity. Despite continued racism and the difficult problems of the black urban underclass, many African Americans of today are doing very well. More blacks than ever before are well-educated, highly paid professionals. These men and women move easily in business and social circles that include many people who are not African American. By moving toward the mainstream of American society, however, some African Americans may feel that they have moved away from their cultural roots. E-mailed lists with items such as "Only Black Folks . . . Have mothers who can use curse words and religion ALL IN ONE SENTENCE"[99] can remind modern-day blacks of their traditions—and help them to take pride in their heritage.

## Looking Back

Finally, studying and retelling black folklore can inspire modern African Americans and bring them to a greater appreciation of their heritage. Virginia Hamilton, for example, inherited her love of American black folktales from her parents. The traditional stories they told while Hamilton was growing up sparked her interest in African American history and culture. Hamilton's grandfather, Levi Perry, moreover, had been a slave in Virginia who had crossed the Ohio River to freedom before the Civil War. Every year, Hamilton reports, Perry sat his children down and told them stories about his life in slavery. His intent was partly to give the children an appreciation for their cultural past and partly to make sure, he explained, "that slavery will never happen to you."[100]

The resurgence of interest in spirituals during the civil rights movement of the 1950s and 1960s provides another example. Following the Civil War, blacks had officially been granted civil rights—full rights of citizenship, such as the ability to vote. In reality, however, whites in the South and elsewhere beat and terrorized African Americans who dared to claim those rights. The civil rights movement was an attempt to establish those basic freedoms for African Americans everywhere. Led primarily by black Southern ministers such as Martin Luther King Jr., the protestors attempted to remain peaceful and focused on their message even as they were reviled and attacked by angry whites opposed to change. It was a difficult task, and it took patience and courage to be an effective civil rights worker.

The civil rights movement relied heavily on music for comfort and for unity. Many of the songs most frequently used by the activists were spirituals. Spirituals containing lines such as "Great day, great day with the righteous marchin'"[101] helped activists recall what they were working for and reassured them that God was on their side. The spirituals that dealt with freedom, moreover, often seemed to apply equally well to the conditions of the 1950s. True, African Americans of the time were not literally enslaved; but the sentiments of a song such as "Go Down, Moses" still seemed appropriate, given the poverty and hopelessness of many blacks.

But the meaning of spirituals in black history was important to civil rights workers, too. Spirituals had helped African Americans through the nightmare of slavery. Now, a century or more afterward, black Americans were engaged in yet another

Activists during the civil rights movement of the 1960s often sang traditional spirituals during marches in order to demonstrate unity and remain inspired.

struggle for freedom, and they looked to their own past to find support. Civil rights leaders took solace and strength from the knowledge that their ancestors had survived the evils of slavery, and they used spirituals to underscore the power of their history and the depth of their ancestors' endurance. "If any single buttress supported Martin Luther King Jr. through his struggle for civil rights, it was the spiritual," writes Daryl Cumber Dance. "In the King movement, as in slavery, the spiritual voiced the plight, communicated the message, comforted the sufferers, uplifted the marchers, and celebrated the victorious."[102]

## Into the Future

Throughout history, black Americans have used folklore to describe, explain, and engage the world around them. In characters such as the proud and courageous John Henry, folklore has given African Americans heroes and role models; in spirituals and the blues, it has provided a way for African Americans to give voice to their sorrows and dreams. By bringing people together and giving them common points of reference, black folklore has reflected the heritage of African Americans and has helped to shape black culture and history. This connection with culture and history has always been an essential characteristic of black folklore.

Another characteristic of black folklore, however, is change. Over the years, African American folk styles have changed again and again, sometimes in small ways, sometimes much more significantly. Spirituals were popular during the early 1800s, the blues a century later. The Br'er Rabbit tales were staples of plantation life; the dozens are much more widespread today. Even the means by which folklore is spread have changed. Once, neighbors gathered on front porches, in marketplaces, and in barbershops to swap riddles and songs. Today, folk material is distributed across the world through books, television programs, compact discs, and the Internet.

Nor have individual songs and stories from African American folklore remained the same. Performers of black American folklore have always been expected to make the material their own—that is, to interpret it according to their own interests and abilities. Each singer or storyteller, therefore, performs songs

African Americans today consider folklore a key element of their cultural identity and traditions.

and stories somewhat differently from others. For that matter, individual storytellers and singers rarely perform the same piece precisely the same way every time. Instead, they tailor each performance to their audience and their mood. In the African American tradition, then, folklore is always changing—and always alive.

How African American folklore will change in the future is impossible to guess. No one knows what methods of transmission will appear next; no one knows what heroes, styles, or forms will capture the imaginations of the next generation of American blacks. If the past is any guide, however, two claims can be made about black folklore in the years to come. The first is that it will not be exactly the same as it is today, or at any point during the past; the folk traditions of African Americans will forever be turning into something new. And the second is that African American folklore will continue to serve as a comfort, a strength, and a reminder of the rich heritage of American blacks.

# Notes

## Introduction: Folklore and African Americans

1. Zora Neale Hurston, *Every Tongue Got to Confess: Negro Folk-Tales from the Gulf States.* New York: HarperCollins, 2001, p. xxiii.

2. Quoted in Daryl Cumber Dance, *From My People: 400 Years of African American Folklore.* New York: W.W. Norton, 2002, p. xxxiii.

3. Virginia Hamilton, *Her Stories.* New York: Blue Sky, 1995, p. 74.

4. Quoted in Dance, *From My People,* p. xxxvii.

5. Dance, *From My People,* pp. xxxiii–xxxiv.

## Chapter One: African American Folk Stories

6. Quoted in Roger D. Abrahams, *Afro-American Folktales.* New York: Pantheon, 1985, p. 66.

7. Julius Lester, *The Tales of Uncle Remus.* New York: Dial, 1987, p. 68.

8. Lester, *The Tales of Uncle Remus,* p. 69.

9. Lester, *The Tales of Uncle Remus,* p. 70.

10. Joel Chandler Harris, *Uncle Remus.* New York: George Routledge and Sons, 1883, p. 128.

11. Harris, *Uncle Remus,* p. 18.

12. Harris, *Uncle Remus,* p. 125.

13. Abrahams, *Afro-American Folktales,* p. 53.

14. Virginia Hamilton, *Bruh Rabbit and the Tar Baby Girl.* New York: Blue Sky, 2003, n.p.

15. Hamilton, *Her Stories,* p. 31.

16. Hamilton, *Her Stories,* p. 32.

17. Virginia Hamilton, *The People Could Fly.* New York: Knopf, 1985, p. 137.

18. Hurston, *Every Tongue Got to Confess,* p. 60.

19. Quoted in John and Alan Lomax, *Best Loved American Folk Songs.* New York: Grosset and Dunlap, 1947, p. 74.

20. Quoted in Dance, *From My People,* p. 609.

21. Hamilton, *Her Stories,* p. 84.

22. Hamilton, *Her Stories,* p. 88.

23. Quoted in Hurston, *Every Tongue Got to Confess,* p. 91.

24. Quoted in Hurston, *Every Tongue Got to Confess,* p. 38.

25. Lester, *The Tales of Uncle Remus,* p. xxi.

## Chapter Two: Folk Songs

26. Lomax and Lomax, *Best Loved American Folk Songs,* p. 334.

27. Frederick Douglass, *Narrative of the Life of Frederick Douglass, an American Slave,* chapter 2. http://sunsite.berkeley.edu/ Literature/Douglass/Auto biography/02.html.

28. Quoted in Dance, *From My People,* p. 84.

29. Quoted in William Francis Allen, Charles Pickard Ware, and Lucy McKim Garrison, *Slave Songs of the United States.* 1867. Reprint. Bedford, MA: Applewood, 1996, p. 82.

30. Quoted in Lomax and Lomax, *Best Loved American Folk Songs,* p. 357.

31. Quoted in Dance, *From My People,* p. 79.

32. Quoted in Dance, *From My People,* p. 96.

33. Quoted in Allen, Ware, and Garrison, *Slave Songs of the United States,* p. 88.

34. Quoted in Allen, Ware, and Garrison, *Slave Songs of the United States,* p. 99.

35. Quoted in Daniel J. Crowley, ed., *African Folklore in the New World.* Austin: University of Texas Press, 1977, p. 29.

36. Lomax and Lomax, *Best Loved American Folk Songs,* p. 225.

37. Quoted in Lomax and Lomax, *Best Loved American Folk Songs,* p. 251.

38. Quoted in Lomax and Lomax, *Best Loved American Folk Songs,* p. 235.

39. Quoted in Carl Sandburg, *The American Songbag.* New York: Harcourt Brace, 1927, p. 25.

40. Quoted in Lomax and Lomax, *Best Loved American Folk Songs,* p. 259.

41. Dance, *From My People,* p. 475.

42. Quoted in Cecil Brown, *Stagolee Shot Billy.* Cambridge, MA: Harvard University Press, 2003, p. 74.

43. Quoted in Abrahams, *Afro-American Folktales,* p. 238.

44. Quoted in Brown, *Stagolee Shot Billy,* p. 3.

45. Quoted in Dance, *From My People,* p. 72.

46. Quoted in Tony Russell, *The Blues.* New York: Schirmer, 1997, p. 19.

47. Quoted in Dance, *From My People,* p. 118.

48. Dance, *From My People,* p. 72.

49. Quoted in Russell, *The Blues,* p. 9.

## Chapter Three: Jokes, Rhymes, and More

50. Hamilton, *The People Could Fly*, p. 159.

51. Quoted in Dance, *From My People*, p. 541.

52. Quoted in Dance, *From My People*, p. 542.

53. Quoted in Hamilton, *The People Could Fly*, p. 157.

54. Quoted in Dance, *From My People*, p. 545.

55. Quoted in Hurston, *Every Tongue Got to Confess*, p. 210.

56. Quoted in Lester, *The Tales of Uncle Remus*, p. 36.

57. Quoted in Hurston, *Every Tongue Got to Confess*, p. 181.

58. Quoted in Dance, *From My People*, p. 551.

59. Quoted in Dance, *From My People*, p. 548.

60. Quoted in Dance, *From My People*, p. 540.

61. Quoted in Hamilton, *The People Could Fly*, pp. 79–80.

62. Quoted in Hurston, *Every Tongue Got to Confess*, p. 146.

63. Harris, *Uncle Remus*, p. 144.

64. Quoted in Dance, *From My People*, p. 507.

65. Quoted in Dance, *From My People*, p. 506.

66. Quoted in Barbara Michels and Bettye White, *Apples on a Stick: The Folklore of Black Children*. New York: Coward-McCann, 1983, p. 12.

67. Quoted in Veronica Chambers, *Double Dutch*. New York: Hyperion Books for Children, 2002, p. 8.

68. Quoted in Chambers, *Double Dutch*, p. 46.

69. Quoted in Michels and White, *Apples on a Stick*, p. 41.

70. Quoted in Dennis Wepman, Ronald B. Newman, and Murray B. Binderman, *The Life: The Lore and Poetry of the Black Hustler*. Philadelphia: University of Pennsylvania Press, 1976, p. 53.

71. Wepman, Newman, and Binderman, *The Life*, p. 7.

72. Quoted in Dance, *From My People*, pp. 653-54.

73. Quoted in Dance, *From My People*, p. 669.

74. Quoted in Snopes.com, "Social Insecurity." www.snopes.com/business/taxes/blackssn.asp.

75. Quoted in Snopes.com, "'Black Tax' Credit." www.snopes.com/business/taxes/blacktax.asp.

## Chapter Four: Roots and Influences

76. Abrahams, *Afro-American Folktales*, p. 4.

77. Quoted in Abrahams, *Afro-American Folktales*, p. 199.

78. Quoted in Roger D. Abrahams, *African Folktales*. New York: Pantheon, 1983, p. 211.

79. Quoted in Hamilton, *The People Could Fly*, p. 63.

80. Allen, Ware, and Garrison, *Slave Songs of the United States*, p. v.

81. Quoted in Dance, *From My People*, p. 77.

82. Quoted in Allen, Ware, and Garrison, *Slave Songs of the United States*, p. vi.

83. Quoted in Lomax and Lomax, *Best Loved American Folk Songs*, p. 335.

84. Quoted in Dance, *From My People*, p. 537.

85. Quoted in Hamilton, *The People Could Fly*, pp. 119–20.

86. Lomax and Lomax, *Best Loved American Folk Songs*, p. 336.

87. Quoted in Hurston, *Every Tongue Got to Confess*, p. 78.

**Chapter Five: Shaping the Black Experience**

88. Hamilton, *Bruh Rabbit and the Tar Baby Girl*.

89. Quoted in Eugene Genovese, *Roll, Jordan, Roll: The World the Slaves Made*. New York: Pantheon, 1972, p. 301.

90. Quoted in Lester, *The Tales of Uncle Remus*, p. 20.

91. Quoted in B.A. Botkin, ed., *Lay My Burden Down: A Folk History of Slavery*. Chicago: University of Chicago Press, 1945, p. 71.

92. Quoted in Abrahams, *Afro-American Folktales*, p. 278.

93. Quoted in Lomax and Lomax, *Best Loved American Folk Songs*, p. 361.

94. Quoted in Julius Lester, *To Be a Slave*. New York: Dial, 1968, p. 83.

95. Quoted in Allen, Ware, and Garrison, *Slave Songs of the United States*, p. xviii.

96. Lester, *The Tales of Uncle Remus*, p. xv.

97. Wepman, Newman, and Binderman, *The Life*, p. 7.

98. Dance, *From My People*, p. 2.

99. Quoted in Dance, *From My People*, p. 659.

100. Quoted in Virginia Hamilton.com, "A Visit with Virginia Hamilton." www.virginiahamilton.com/pages/biostuff.htm.

101. Quoted in Lomax and Lomax, *Best Loved American Folk Songs*, p. 340.

102. Dance, *From My People*, p. 71.

# For More Information

## Books

Roger D. Abrahams, *African Folktales.* New York: Pantheon, 1983. A collection of traditional folk narratives from Africa, including quite a few from West Africa.

Roger D. Abrahams, *Afro-American Folktales.* New York: Pantheon, 1985. Stories collected from blacks in the United States as well as in the islands of the Caribbean. The collection includes stories from the nineteenth century and a few specific to more recent years as well.

William Francis Allen, Charles Pickard Ware, and Lucy McKim Garrison, *Slave Songs of the United States.* 1867. Reprint. Bedford, MA: Applewood. A wonderful collection of songs, most but not all spirituals, sung by slaves during the Civil War. The authors were Northerners who notated the lyrics and melodies of the songs and published them with some commentary.

Cecil Brown, *Stagolee Shot Billy.* Cambridge, MA: Harvard University Press, 2003. The definitive book about Stagolee—the myth, the songs, and the real people behind the story.

Veronica Chambers, *Double Dutch.* New York: Hyperion Books for Children, 2002. A book with illustrations, quotes, and information about the jump-rope style known as double Dutch, which is very popular among many African American girls. It includes examples of double Dutch rhymes.

Stephen Currie, *The African American Religious Experience.* Detroit, Lucent, 2008. Information about black religious life over the years, with sections on spirituals and the influence of religion on black culture.

Daryl Cumber Dance, *From My People: 400 Years of African American Folklore.* New York: W.W. Norton, 2002. A remarkable sourcebook filled with all kinds of folklore from the African American tradition, together with commentary by the compiler.

Virginia Hamilton, *Her Stories.* New York: Blue Sky, 1995. A well-illustrated collection of folktales from various parts of the black American tradition. These stories focus on strong female characters. Hamilton, a noted children's author, provides information about each story and a valuable introduction as well.

Virginia Hamilton, *The People Could Fly.* New York: Knopf, 1985. Another collection of black folktales collected and retold by Hamilton.

Joel Chandler Harris, *Uncle Remus.* New York: George Routledge and Sons, 1883. This is the original collection of Br'er Rabbit tales. It can be difficult to read because Harris writes mainly in heavy dialect, but Harris had an excellent ear and captured the rhythms of black speech quite well.

Zora Neale Hurston, *Every Tongue Got to Confess: Negro Folk-Tales from the Gulf States.* New York: HarperCollins, 2001. Hurston was an author and scholar who collected a large number of black folktales during the late 1920s. This volume includes many of those stories and provides excellent insight into the themes of black folklore at the time.

Charles Johnson and Patricia Smith, *Africans in America.* New York: Harcourt Brace, 1998. A rich volume describing slavery in America, from the earliest years through the Civil War. It provides some examples of folklore and a good deal of useful background information as well.

Julius Lester, *The Tales of Uncle Remus.* New York: Dial, 1987. Lester is a well-known writer; these are his very enjoyable retellings of some of the Br'er Rabbit tales published a century earlier by Joel Chandler Harris.

Julius Lester, *To Be a Slave.* New York: Dial, 1968. A short book describing slavery in the words of the slaves—a rarity for its time. It includes commentary and some material on folklore as well as valuable background information on African American history and culture.

John and Alan Lomax, *Best Loved American Folk Songs.* New York: Grosset and Dunlap, 1947. An excellent collection of traditional American song lyrics and music, including quite a few examples of spirituals and blues. The authors also provide important background information for each song and group of songs.

Barbara Michels and Bettye White, *Apples on a Stick: The Folklore of Black Children.* New York: Coward-McCann, 1983. This book is a collection of what the authors call "playground poetry"—rhymes and chants frequently used by black children in Houston during the early 1980s.

Tony Russell, *The Blues.* New York: Schirmer, 1997. A well-illustrated history of the blues, with plenty of information on blues singers, blues songs, and recordings of the blues.

Carl Sandburg, *The American Songbag.* New York: Harcourt Brace, 1927. This work is much like the Lomax collection of songs listed above. Compared to the Lomax collection, this volume includes fewer spirituals and more blues and work songs; Sandburg's commentary is usually light and not terribly informative.

Dennis Wepman, Ronald B. Newman, and Murray B. Binderman, *The Life: The Lore and Poetry of the Black Hustler.* Philadelphia: University of Pennsylvania Press, 1976. This book contains examples of toasts, together with lots of valuable background information. It also includes a very helpful glossary.

## Other Materials

*The Adventures of Brer Rabbit.* DVD. Universal City, CA: Universal Pictures,

2006. A filmed retelling of some of the best-known Br'er Rabbit stories.

*Desperate Man Blues.* CD. Atlanta: Dust to Digital, 2006. A collection of early blues recordings, including some of the best-known blues artists of the first half of the 1900s.

*Wade in the Water.* Vol. 1. *African American Spirituals: The Concert Tradition.* CD. Washington: Smithsonian Folkways, 1994. Versions of traditional African American spirituals performed by individual singers and choirs.

*Yoruba Drums from Benin, West Africa.* CD. Washington: Smithsonian Folkways, 1996. Traditional drum music from West Africa, played by modern performers. One of many excellent recordings of traditional West African music; demonstrates the African roots of African American music.

*Zora Is My Name!* DVD. Thousand Oaks, CA: Monterey Video, 2006. A film of a stage play about the life and work of author and folklorist Zora Neale Hurston. It features many of the folktales she collected.

# Index

# Picture Credits

Cover: Library of Congress

AP Images, 51, 83

The Art Archive, 15

The Art Archive/Culver Pictures, 28, 72

The Art Archive/John Meek, 14, 78

Spencer Arnold/Getty Images, 60

© Bettmann/Corbis, 10, 32

Burke/Triolo Productions/Jupiterimages, 88

© Danita Delimont/Alamy, 40

Bernard Gotfryd/Hulton Archives/Getty Images, 37

Hulton Archive/Getty Images, 17, 61

Library of Congress, 19, 35, 50, 76

© Mary Evans Picture Library/The Imageworks, 69

© North Wind Picture Archives, 30

Michael Ochs Archives/Getty Images, 39

© Steve Prezant/Corbis, 48

© Bob Sacha/Corbis, 81

Kurt Severin/Getty Images, 86

Time & Life Pictures/Mansell/Getty Images, 29

© 2008/Jupiterimages 45, 55

# About the Author

Stephen Currie is the author of dozens of books, educational materials, and magazine articles, including several other volumes in the Lucent Library of Black History series. He is also a part-time teacher. He lives in New York State with his family and enjoys kayaking, bicycling, and snowshoeing.